The Five Attributes of a Church in Revival

The Five Attributes of a Church in Revival

David E. Carr

New Wine Press

New Wine Ministries
PO Box 17
Chichester
West Sussex
United Kingdom
PO19 2AW

ISBN 1-903725-65-8

Typeset by CRB Associates, Reepham, Norfolk
Cover design by CCD, www.ccdgroup.co.uk
Printed in Malta

Contents

Endorsements

"David Carr is a man who seeks after the heart of God. David spends his life seeking to keep in step with the Holy Spirit and to live in the blessing of revival. And then with God's favour, he calls out for us to join him in the blessing."
Rev. Roger W. Haskins, Jr.
Bishop, Free Methodist Church of North America

"This book gives clear insights into what may help and hinder revival in our churches, but be warned: it's no easy 'how to' manual – it's real, challenging, thought provoking, hard-hitting and will leave you both longing for more of God and aware of the cost that revival comes at. I wholeheartedly recommend not only reading this book, but letting its wisdom impact your life."
Mike Pilavachi, Soul Survivor

"This stunning book is a straight-talking, hard-hitting, 'Back to Basics' trumpet call to battle-weary churches seeking revival today. Bouncer turned pastor, David Carr speaks and writes with prophetic punch and power. A big man in every way, his heart for the whole Body of Christ beats passionately on every page. I loved this book for its humorous, sharp, insightful

and high-octane encouragement. It will energize receptive leaders and churches everywhere in their hot pursuit of God."
Greg Haslam, Minister, Westminster Chapel, London

"We hear a lot about the 'emerging church', but we don't quite know what is emerging! Dr David Carr's book warmed my heart and reminded me that the Church that emerged after Pentecost was marked by 'great power' and 'great grace'. I encourage every church leader to read this book because the Church urgently needs to embrace these attributes."
Canon J. John

Foreword

It is difficult to describe the multi-talented ministry of
David Carr. His personality and versatility beggar
description. He has exhibited a truly charismatic
ministry with a deep dependence upon the authority of
the Word of God and the Holy Spirit.

David is a true motivator with a discerning eye for
those who desire to discover and develop their gifting
and to exercise ministry within the Body of Christ.
Many have been mentored by him and have taken their
functional places within local churches.

David's unpredictability in every situation has been
a fascinating feature of his public and private activity.
The element of surprise and spontaneity sometimes
with ecstatic movements of unplanned intrusion is
generally present. His ability to shock and challenge is
contained within any situation.

The life and ministry of this man of God symbolise
the meaning of true worship. He jealously guards the
truth of the importance of the anointing and seeks to
inspire a belief in the absolute centrality of Jesus
Christ. His exercise of spiritual gifts, particularly
personal prophecy, has brought an accurate dimension
of the Spirit's discernment wherever he has ministered.

David's belief that the Church has a commission to
present the gospel to the world has taken him,

members of his leadership team and members of his church, to many parts of the world. Furthermore, he typifies the passions for revival and renewal espoused by the great spiritual reformers of the past and desires to see the traditions of the Church superseded by a radical, relevant and revolutionary brand of New Testament Church.

David's sensitivity as a pastor is demonstrated in the love and care he has given to the local church. He has taught, discipled and counselled extensively and no one is exempted from his concern and compassion, sometimes at considerable personal cost.

His difficulty in being contained and constrained within the strict boundaries of denominational life is well known. Maybe it is because he desires to be free to move among the wider Body of Christ. It is certain that the Church of God will continue to be blessed by the dynamic ministry of this apostolic figure.

Rev. Eldin R. Corsie
Former General Superintendent
of Elim Pentecostal Churches and
Senior Pastor of Kensington Temple
London, UK

Introduction

Today, many people are asking the question: "What do we need to do in order to see the Holy Spirit visit our local church in power?" There is scarcely a believer anywhere who doesn't want to see a greater manifestation of God's power; to see people healed, delivered, miraculously swept into the kingdom; to see the Church functioning as it should. And there is a constant interest in past revivals – what was the spark that triggered them, what characterized them? – as we hope to precipitate a revival in our present day.

I believe there are five vital aspects that characterized every historic revival, and these are the subject of this book. But in my writing I am not looking back in history, I am looking forward. I believe that if we, as a body of believers, focus our attention on these five areas we will be *positioning* ourselves for revival. They are five signs that indicate what a church in revival will look like.

It is not my intention in this book to act as a consultant to the Body of Christ by examining and giving a diagnosis on the health of the Church, either local or national. Nor do I intend to give a fail-safe formula for success. I don't believe one exists! My desire is to unpack and help us to understand these five attributes that always seem to accompany a genuine move of God, regardless of stream or denomination. This is important, because it is not methods or models, but *principles* that are the basic foundations for the building of blessed churches. Spiritual ingredients of the highest quality are needed if we are to see a complete and lasting Holy Spirit-inspired Church in our nation today.

Unless local churches, or even national movements, have been born and sustained by vision and principles, the struggle to be relevant to both God and our community is immense. A desperation to see results has caused many an eldership to look nationally or globally for help and guidance, instead of heavenwards. I believe the G12s, Torontos, Pensacolas and Willow Creeks of the world to be powerful outworkings of God's power in their particular location, but trying to copy what is happening there and importing it to your local church/town is not likely to bring the results you hope for. Many churches, after much commitment and effort, have been disappointed that the dynamic growth patterns they expected have not emerged by emulating these models.

It is certain that basic truths must be transferable, but culture, the state of a nation's spirituality, and the possibility of an open heaven over a specific geographical area will always be driving factors in any outpouring of the Spirit that exceeds our normal experience. In other words, Bogota is not always synonymous with Bognor Regis!

Believe it or not, there are fellowships in our nation that came into being for different reasons other than

Holy Spirit-led vision. Church splits, denominational dictates, and lack of apostolic input are just a few of the many reasons. I don't intend that as a sweeping generalization or to cause anyone offence. My point is, it will be hard to see a reviving move of God amongst a community of people that He didn't birth!

Having been an Overseer for many years I can concur that some churches should be closed down and the people released to attend a church of true vision and destiny that possesses the gifting and ability to change the society in which they live. People may protest at that saying, "The Lord has told us to keep the doors open." Why, if the walls have fallen down?!

I want to pause for a moment and share with you the vision and principles that underpin our own fellowship in the heart of England. This is not to say we have "got it right" – we are pilgrims charting the course we believe God has laid before us. But I hope it will illustrate the principle of building from vision upwards to achieve your goals.

God has given our body of believers a vision to see 7,000 born-again, Spirit-filled believers meeting together within a network of congregations in the heart of England. Our desire is to be prophetic and holy in leadership, lifestyle, worship, preaching and prayer. We are a church that cares for and loves people (Matthew 25), that is relevant to all ages (including children and youth). We desire to change and affect our community, to be multicultural, and to train and equip people for the work of the ministry.

I summarize our aims as follows:

- To convey the Christian gospel in a way that is relevant to our community
- To equip Christians to minister in the community in word and deed
- To be relevant and to meet the needs of the poor, homeless, disadvantaged and those with life addictions
- To be guided by the Holy Spirit to fulfil the vision of the Church
- To establish congregations and Family Care Centres throughout the heart of England
- To see our church continue to increase and be relevant to people of all nations, all abilities, all gifting and all needs
- To work closely with other churches, organisations, and local and national government, that we may lead a peaceable life

From that base our structure is built. At the heart of all we do are our principles, but without structure we will never see an outpouring of the Spirit. Remember the story of Elisha in 2 Kings 4:6 God wanted to provide an abundance of oil for a needy widow, so Elisha commanded her to go to her neighbours and ask to borrow as many pots as she could get her hands on. However, she didn't do it. Instead she immediately went home and shut the door! God still multiplied the oil, but after she had filled the few pots she had, the oil stopped. If she had obeyed God's command to the letter, she would have had a greater abundance of oil.

So it is with us if we fail to obey God's commands and try to build church on faulty foundations. So many churches are desperately hungry and thirsty for the Holy Spirit, and yet are not actually listening to what the Spirit is saying. We don't want the flow of oil to be short lived for lack of obedience.

True moves of God are individual in appearance, yet fundamental characteristics are seen beneath the signs and wonders. At this time little Holy Spirit revival is taking place in the UK or in Europe. Since our culture is steeped in Greek thinking – a cerebrally-orientated philosophy that analyses and disseminates Scripture until the anointing is squeezed out of it – there is perhaps little wonder that we see scant change.

Why do you want to see revival?

But the bigger questions is: why do people constantly long for a revival? The following are questions that I always ask leaders who talk about revival:

1. Why do you want to see a revival?
2. What do you think revival is?
3. Can you cope with the cost?

The answer to the first question is not as obvious as it seems. It can range from (1) to bring people into the church (2) because our church is dead! (3) to become the bride that Jesus intended us to be. Personally I identify most with No. 3. An outpouring of the Spirit is not for any peripheral purpose other than the perfecting and equipping of His Church.

My early Christian life had its foundations in the Pentecostal movement. Thank God for Pentecostalism's biblical teaching and access to the Holy Spirit. Yet, its obsession with tongues to the detriment of other facets of the gifts of the Spirit, has diverted many people away from developing a true and meaningful relationship with Father God.

I, like the apostle Paul, venture into the tongues controversy with the credentials, *"I speak with tongues more than you all"* (1 Corinthians 14:18). People tell me that I speak in many known languages and I have seen people weep before God after hearing me speak over them in their native tongue. I once led a young Satanist to the Lord, seeing her delivered from evil spirits, saved and filled with the Holy Spirit, all through the act of speaking over her for fifteen minutes in tongues. I was told later that I had spoken perfect French. A French-speaking bystander was both amazed and frightened as she knew I had no knowledge whatsoever of the language. I recount this story in order to say to you: if we want to live in revival, the question we should be asking each other is not, "Do you speak in tongues?", but, "Do you know the Holy Spirit?"

In Acts chapter 2, although the outpouring of the Holy Spirit at Pentecost was accompanied by an outbreak of speaking in tongues, there were other prerequisites that superseded it. The tongues were a sign that the outpouring had come, but there were at least four factors that led up to that visible manifestation that we need to consider:

1. Obedience

Jesus instructed His disciples,

> *"Behold, I send the Promise of My Father upon you; but tarry in the city of Jerusalem until you are endued with power from on high."*
>
> (Luke 24:49)

The disciples were told to "tarry" – to sit down, not to move away, in modern language, or "Don't do a runner" (the Brummie version!). "If you will wait obediently," Jesus said, "then you will be *endued* (literally, wrapped up as in a garment) with power." So the first requirement for a personal or corporate move of God is simple obedience! Mary the mother of Jesus put it succinctly when she instructed the stewards at the wedding, "Whatever he tells you to do, do it" – a statement that preceded Jesus' first miracle. If a Christian or a church lives in disobedience, then all the scripture in the world will not engage the hand of Almighty God.

The disciples received the command to "wait" until the right time. We often miss the supernatural through not obeying simple commands from God. A simple story illustrates the fact that not obeying God can be potentially life-threatening. Once I was travelling home from a preaching engagement in Rotherham, South Yorkshire. The road was clear, the hour late. I was driving at 70 miles per hour in the outside lane, having just overtaken a truck, when the Holy Spirit spoke to me saying, "Move into the slow land and cut your speed to 50 now." I looked in my mirror but I couldn't see any reason why I should do it. Then the Lord spoke again: "The enemy of your life desires to kill you." That got my attention, so I obeyed and moved into the slow lane, dropping down to 50 miles per hour. Seconds later a car came from nowhere and passed me at high speed, lost control for no apparent reason, hit the crash barrier and completely flipped over. This car literally bounced over my car and careered over the top of the grass bank that flanked the carriageway, disappearing into the darkness. In the pitch blackness I climbed the bank and found the wrecked car. A young lady was trapped inside, sobbing but relatively unscathed. "Why am I not dead?" she cried. "Because I was obedient to God," I answered truthfully.

The moral of the story is: "Do whatever He (the Holy Spirit) tells you to do." Obedience is the first step that leads to an outpouring of the Spirit.

2. Of one accord

The disciples were said to be of "one accord" (Greek: *homothumadon*). It means to be unanimous, to establish a mutual covenant, to be in agreement with one mind and purpose, in harmony. The Bible teaches that unity brings a blessing:

> *"Behold, how good and how pleasant it is*
> *For brethren to dwell together in unity!"*
>
> (Psalm 133:1)

Jesus spoke of being one with Father and expressed His desire for us to be in the very same covenant of unity:

"And the glory which You gave Me I have given them, that they may be one just as We are one..."
(John 17:22)

The presence of true spiritual unity is a prerequisite to any revival. The Christian community is littered with the remains of broken relationships. The causing or taking of offence has led to many Christians leaving perfectly good churches where they belonged. They have not been called out for service, they have simply walked out of the service! The sin of offence is prolific among the ecclesia. Often the world must see the Church like a collection of primitive tribal factions, more preoccupied with fighting each other than unifying against the enemy!

With unity comes power. When Sir William Wallace of Elerslie united the clans of Scotland in circa 1270, they struck fear into their enemies, especially King Edward of England. The uniting of the clans gave considerable authority to their plan for a totally independent Scotland. It was only when the unity held that victory was achieved.

General George A. Custer made a decision to attack and fight the Sioux Indians at the Little Big Horn. In a short time all of the 264 troops under Custer's command had died, including five members of Custer's own family. The Sioux had united under the leadership of Chief Sitting Bull and Crazy Horse.

These two historic events are but a simple illustration of the force that is generated by unity and

of working together to achieve a single purpose.
That which cannot be conquered by individualism is
conquerable by unity. Remember, if God is for us,
who can be against us?

3. Righteousness

As the disciples waited in obedience, all in one accord,
eventually the mighty rushing wind of the Spirit blew
through the room where they were gathered. The flow
of Holy Spirit power removes the deadness of fallen
creation leaving it naked, yet prepared for clothing in
power. The image of a tree comes to mind, with its
lifeless leaves being driven from the branches so that
new, abundant life can grow in its place. First comes
the blossom, then the fruit, for the sweet act of
adoration – the aroma of praise – always precedes the
rush of power. When the Spirit comes upon us, it is our
heart – our central, emotional identity – that is swept
clean by the rushing wind and we are purified. As one
hymn writer put it, describing our need to be clothed
in the Spirit: "Naked, come to Thee for dress".[1] We
need to be dressed by God in a robe of righteousness –
to have no impure motives.

The wind in the Upper Room was no natural
phenomena, it was heaven sent. This hymn by Edwin
Hatch aptly describes the Spirit's effect:

> Breathe on me, Breath of God,
> Fill me with life anew,
> That I may love what Thou dost love,
> And do what Thou wouldst do.

Breathe on me, Breath of God,
Until my heart is pure
Until with Thee I will one will,
To do or to endure.

Breathe on me, Breath of God,
Till I am wholly Thine,
Until this earthly part of me
Glows with Thy fire divine.

Breathe on me, Breath of God,
So shall I never die,
But live with Thee the perfect life
Of Thine eternity.[2]

4. Holiness

Fire fell on the disciples, tongues of fire resting on
each one of them, illustrating the fact that the Holy
Spirit's anointing, available to all, is essential to the
individual. He is the very pruning, purging, cleansing,
purifying, energising presence of God. The mark of true
holiness is seen; God's voice is heard, yet we are not
consumed. General Booth, the Salvationist leader,
believed it was only by the "blood" of Jesus Christ in
His redemptive sacrifice on Calvary and the "fire" of
the Holy Spirit, that the vilest unbeliever could be
saved and know the power of His holiness.

On a Sunday morning on 2nd September 1666, the
Great Fire of London began. The blaze devastated an
area of one-and-a-half miles by half a mile – 373 acres
inside the city walls and 63 acres beyond. Eighty-seven
churches including St Paul's Cathedral and 13,200

houses lay in destruction. Amazingly, official reports
say that only six people died. What good came out of
such a fire? Well, it purged the city of the Great
Plague. In the previous year 17,440 people, out of a
population of 90,000, had died from the plague.[3]

The fire may have destroyed that which can be
counted as temporal, but it purged the disease –
human life was saved by the fire. Booth understood
the significance of "Blood and Fire". He has seen a
spiritual "fire of London" in the realm of the Spirit.

After these four criteria had been fulfilled, it was
then that the Spirit was outpoured on the day of
Pentecost and many spoke with other tongues as the
Spirit gave them utterance. It was this phenomenon
that drew the crowds to see and hear what was going
on. The multiracial gathering could hear men praising
God in their own language. For me, this answers the
remaining two questions I posed earlier: What do you
think revival is? And, Can you cope with the cost? The
cost of submitting to the Holy Spirit is high. When you
determine to obediently follow the vision Jesus has
given you, the cost of the rejection of others can also
be high. Notice in Acts that not all of the onlookers
marvelled at what they saw and heard, some mocked
or were perplexed.

A genuine outpouring of the Spirit always leads to a
welcoming of the prophetic and to systematic biblical
preaching. Peter addressed the historic teachings of the
Jews and then proclaimed the prophetic revelation that
Jesus was the long-awaited Messiah, crucified, risen
and the ascended coming King. The response was
immediate, "What must we do to be saved?" Healings,

signs and wonders, the preaching of the word, ministry to the poor, were all established by the early Church following this great outpouring of the Holy Spirit.

It is the fruit of this outpouring that I want to focus on for the remainder of this book. It falls into five sections, each dealing with a particular attribute of a revival church: Worship, Word, Wonders, Wealth and Wellbeing. The first section on worship is the longest, since worship must always be pre-eminent in the Church. It's primarily what mankind exists for! Focusing on establishing these five areas as the foundations of your church will, I believe, position you for revival. I pray they will serve as a wake-up call to us all. Ezekiel's call to his nation is appropriate to all of us today. Let the dry bones live!

Notes _____

1. Rev. Augustus Montague Toplady, *Rock of Ages*, circa 1775.
2. "Breathe on Me, Breath of God", Edwin Hatch (1835–1889).
3. Source: www.angliacampus.com

Worship – Part 1

A single statement at the end of Exodus chapter 4 has always been significant to me when it comes to discussing the topic of worship. Significant, because it points to one of the root causes of *why* we are motivated to worship God.

Exodus 4 recounts Moses' commissioning to leadership and his early dealings with the people of Israel as their newly appointed leader. As an aside, it is interesting to notice the detail of Aaron's commissioning alongside that of Moses'. Aaron went out into the desert to see Moses and Moses relayed to him all that God had revealed to him, unfolding God's strategy for the deliverance of His people. The visionary told the pastor what he had heard from God and then the pastor told the people. It provides us with a model for leadership which I believe would serve us well in the Church today. Too many church leadership structures are being strangled by democracy!

Aaron assembled all the people and told them about the liberation that God was going to bring to them. They were a really motley crew! Much of the time they didn't know what they were doing and the Bible records that they were mumblers and grumblers who regularly protested about the things God commanded them to do. From this I draw the parallel that if you are a visionary leader with a mandate from God, seeking to position your church for revival, then you won't always do things that everybody likes! However, we read in verses 29–31 that Moses and Aaron gathered the Israelite elders together to tell them all that God was going to do and "... *performed the signs before the people, **and they believed**...* " (NIV, emphasis added).

> **"Belief is key. Unless you believe where God is directing you as a church, then you're not going!"**

Belief is key. Unless you believe where God is directing you as a church, then you're not going! You have to believe that God wants you to be a worshipping church; a church of the Word; a church that can supply wealth to meet the needs of the people, to help people who are desperate and needy. Once you know you have heard God's mandate for you as a body of believers, you must believe it and refuse to let go!

Now we come to the statement itself in verse 31:

> *"... when they heard that the* LORD *had visited the children of Israel and that He had looked on their affliction, then they bowed their heads and they worshipped."*

Although they were given to much moaning and groaning, when the Israelites heard that the Lord had actually come amongst them and had seen their affliction – their sickness and disease, their loneliness, their lack of resources – and not only come amongst them but seen their affliction – they fell down and worshipped Him!

Although we know from Scripture that man's primary function is to worship God and enjoy His presence – in other words we have a responsibility to worship – time and again what motivates us to worship Him is His love for us – His interest and concern for our personal wellbeing. When you believe that God is in the house and He is looking at your affliction; when you are sitting at home feeling alone, but know that God sees your loneliness and cares for you – then you want to worship Him!

When God visits your house

I'm reminded of the story of a woman who came to talk to me at the end of a service when I was speaking in another town. She was excited because God had "visited" her and she wanted to tell someone about it. She picked on me because she felt I would believe her! She told me that her husband had died recently and so she was all alone. To make matters worse, she lived half a mile down a dirt track in a very isolated part of Bodmin Moor. She had no friends or relatives around and as winter arrived, she felt scared and cut off. At night it was pitch black on the Moor with no street lighting. "Pastor David," she said to me, "you can imagine that most of the time I lived in fear." I could understand very well. I know plenty of men who would have had a shotgun and a pair of Rottweilers handy in that situation, let alone a frightened widow!

So this dear lady wept before the Lord and said, "Lord, I'm all alone. I've got nobody. If something ever went wrong there would be nobody to help me!" And at that moment the Lord spoke to her and said, "Look out of your window." Wondering whether she had heard correctly and peering hesitantly out of the window, she was amazed at what she saw. There were four enormous angels standing there, one positioned at each corner of the house! God spoke to her again and said, "Is that enough protection for you?" This is the kind of thing that can happen when you realise that God is visiting your house and taking notice of your affliction!

Exodus 4:31 tells us that in reverence to God the people *"bowed their heads and worshipped"*. In most modern church services we don't think very much about coming to bow down before we worship God, and yet the act of bowing down and worshipping is mentioned ninety-four times in the Old Testament. Some people think that bowing our heads before God is a kind of church tradition, and many churches in the renewal movement tend to resist being tied down by tradition – but no, it's there in the Bible! I don't ever want to be legalistic about it, but I think it would be good if people came into church and bowed their heads in worship occasionally before the service began. Sometimes evangelicals can be the most stubborn about these things: "Nobody's going to tell me to bow my head; nobody's going to tell me to put my hands in the air!" Well, no one should have to tell you in the first place! The fact that anyone has to prompt these things shows how disrespectful some people are of God. If we truly are a worshipping church then we will bow our heads in reverence.

Man's desire to worship

Isaiah chapter 44 talks about the foolishness of idolatry – worshipping someone or something other than God Himself. The fact is, we all worship, believer and unbeliever alike. But who or what will we worship? This passage makes clear the futility of man's efforts to create idols for himself to worship. It illustrates the irony of idolatry by explaining how a man will plant a pine tree, and after the passage of time will chop it down to use as wood for his fire. With the wood burning he will warm himself and also bake bread or roast meat over it. Yet, with the leftovers of the same wood he will carve the image of an idol and fall down and worship it! How stupid!

> **"We have become skilled at not allowing God to infiltrate the parts of our lives we don't want Him to interfere with."**

Inside every man and woman there is the ability and desire, not just to worship, but to *fall down* before that which we worship. This is not some kind of charismatic mania, but an instinctive desire placed in man at creation.

The reason that we find it hard to worship is because we don't fully know the presence of God. I wish I had a pound for every time someone has said to me, "But it's not part of British culture to express ourselves like that David!" or "We're not expressive/emotional people!' I have always found such statements bewildering, but especially so when I was involved in the football business. My reply would always be, "You are expressive enough at 3.00pm on a Saturday afternoon! ... You're emotional when your team is in a cup match! ... You express yourself freely enough when you're at a disco or on a pub crawl!" So why aren't we the same in church? Why? Because we have become skilled at not allowing God to infiltrate the parts of our lives we don't want Him to interfere with.

A warning against idols

The irony of idolatry is: how can anything you can control be a god? Isaiah 44:19 says,

> *"No one considers in his heart,*
> *Nor is there knowledge nor understanding to say,*
> *'I have burned half of it in the fire,*
> *Yes, I have also baked bread on its coals;*
> *I have roasted meat and eaten it;*

*And shall I make the rest of it an abomination?
Shall I fall down before a block of wood?' "*

In other words, most of the time we haven't got the
brains to work out that something we can use and
abuse couldn't possibly be a god to us! You can't
submit to something that can easily be brought
under your control! That's why we worship God,
because He is exceedingly beyond our ability to
control or even understand! That's the reason why
some people prefer religion to real Christianity. They
like religion because it helps them to contain God
within their religious rituals – at least in their minds.
When God turns up in the house however, and you've
got no control over what's happening, people get
frightened.

Aren't we stupid? We can control money and yet we
try to make it our god. We can control drink, but it
becomes our god. We can control our sex drive, but it
becomes our god. We can control relationships and
marriages, but we make them into gods too! The
danger inherent in making gods of these things is that
if we persist in following them, eventually God "gives
us over" to them. Then, that which we once controlled,
controls us. If you persist in making sex or drugs your
god, then eventually you will find yourself in bondage
and under submission to those things.

Thankfully, God never puts us under submission like
that. I don't worship Jesus because I *have to*. I'm a free
man! I worship Jesus because *I choose* to worship Him.
After all He has done for me, you couldn't stop me
from worshipping Him if you tried!

Kissing the hand of God

In the New Testament on fifty-nine occasions the word worship is rendered with the meaning, "to kiss the hand or the ground". I always thought that when the Pope flew Aer Lingus, disembarked the plane and kissed the ground, it was because he was either frightened of flying or relieved he'd arrived in one piece! But no, it's an act of worship and submission to God. In a similar vein, that is the reason why people used to kiss the Pope's or the monarch's ring – it was an act of reverence and submission. This act demonstrates that you are placing yourself under their authority. That's why the New Testament paints the picture of bowing down and "kissing" the hand of God. In our worship we are saying to the Lord, "I totally submit myself to your authority." In biblical times people even went so far as to lie on the floor and allow a person in authority over them to place their foot on their head. It meant, "You actually have the authority to squash me if you want to, I am so yielded to you, but nevertheless I am coming under submission to your rulership."

When we worship God we are not just saying "thank you for saving me", although thankfulness to God should be an ever present factor, rather we are submitting our worldly, arrogant flesh to His lordship and the rule of His Spirit. But it goes even deeper than that. At least twenty-four times in the New Testament the word "worship", directed at both God and Jesus, is an acknowledgement of the simple fact that He is God.

So when Jehovah's Witnesses claim that Jesus was never worshipped as God, they are wrong!

> **"Any church that is beginning to move in revival will increasingly know the fear of God in their worship."**

Worship has a yet deeper emotional experience at its core, because it means "to venerate, to hold in awe, to have a holy fear of". Any church that is beginning to move in revival will increasingly know the fear of God in their worship. They will be concerned with "venerating" Jesus – recognizing Him for who He is: God the Son. We must hold Jesus in awe as never before and that should have a very direct effect on our worship, the songs we sing, the way we conduct ourselves in God's house.

Your work is worship to God!

Looking at the roots of the word for "worship" you may be surprised to learn that it is closely linked to the concept of "work". In other words, our worship life is not something that is separate from our other daily activities. Just the opposite is true! They are intrinsically linked. People have said to me in the past, "Pastor Dave, I long to be in full-time ministry because I find it impossible to worship/serve God at work." No!

According to the Bible your work *is* an act of worship to God. Tomorrow when you arrive at the office or factory, or school, or college ... you will be worshipping God with your hands, with your attitude to your work and the way in which you interact with others. Biblical work is worship!

I want to belong to the kind of church where everyone is working; where the vast majority, unless there is a good reason why, have jobs and are able to glorify God in their places of work. How can we as believers be salt and light in the earth unless we are examples of godliness in the marketplace? What a wonderful example to others when they see your lifestyle and think, "Hey, they seem to work very differently from everyone else!" because you are truthful, honest, you're a grafter, you don't cheat, you don't take sick days when you don't feel like going in. I want our church to have a reputation that grabs the attention of local employers, so that they begin to say to potential employees, "Oh, you go to Renewal church do you? Well you must strive for excellence then. If we take you on we're sure the business will be run right." Why? Because you belong to a church that believes every facet of your life is part of your worship.

Many churches today are in danger of losing the sense of the awesomeness of God. I want to rid the Church of the kind of attitude that has crept in that says, "I might go to church on Sunday if I feel like it, but I've had a really busy week ... " or, "I'd like to go to church, but I've got a report that needs to be in by Monday ... " Listen folks, God doesn't need us to do Him a favour by gracing the church with our presence!

He is doing us a favour by letting us in! I can't stand it when people say, "I was busy last week so I couldn't come to church." I doubt there are many people in my church busier than I am, but even when I was running the church and still continuing my career in business, Sunday was always set apart as God's day. People would try to move heaven and earth, but no one could have my day with Jesus!

If you have to constantly invade the day that should be set apart for worshipping God then you had better alter the structure of your week! This isn't legalism, it's biblical! Can you imagine any husband saying to his wife, "I'm a bit busy with work this week dear, I'll be home next week if I can fit you in"? In no time at all you wouldn't have a marriage if you behaved like that. In fact, when you did eventually arrive home, you'd have to approach the house with caution, because there would be a saucepan coming your way and it wouldn't have your dinner in it!

> **"If you have to constantly invade the day that should be set apart for worshipping God then you had better alter the structure of your week!"**

You may think I'm presenting an extreme example, but I know many Christians who, because they are busy, fit God into their lives at their convenience, perhaps once a month in between the golf club, the caravan and the job. It worries me when Christians have little desire to be in the house of God. If we were truly on fire for Jesus then no one would be able to keep us away.

When I was still involved in the football business I was the agent for Brian Robson and had the task of assisting with his signing to Manchester United, in the days when Ron Atkinson was managing the club. A deal had been in the offing for a while, but when I eventually got the phone call telling me it was time to sign the contracts, it conflicted with a prior appointment I had.

"David, you've got to be at the Man United ground by 10.30am because the press will be there. Ron Atkinson is ready to sign him," said the anxious voice on the phone.

"Sorry, I can't be there at 10.30am," I said. "I'm doing a harvest festival at Greswold Primary School."

Totally perplexed, my colleague responded, "You didn't hear me Dave! You've got to be there then because the press will be there. It's going to be announced on the lunchtime news!"

"Tough!" I said. "I'm going to take an assembly for five-year-olds at Greswold School because I promised them I'd be there. You're going to have to wait!"

So, they waited. An announcement was made on the lunchtime news that day that, "There has been a slight technical hitch with Brian Robson's signing. There will be a full report on the five o'clock news"!

So I did my assembly and then drove up to Manchester. The champagne was on ice ready for the event, the press were gathered; everybody was there, and in I walked with my briefcase. No doubt people were thinking, "He must have been off signing someone else before he came here!" But, no! I was busy telling five-year-olds about Jesus because that was my priority! And Brian Robson still was signed to Manchester United and went on to captain England. The principle is: seek first the kingdom of God and His righteousness and everything you need will be added to you as well. A lifestyle of worshipping Jesus and putting Him first must be our priority.

My work has always been a part of my worship. I was often asked, "Pastor Dave, how do you manage your life working in football *and* being a pastor?" People who think like that are asking the wrong question. God doesn't want us to split our lives in two and separate the sacred from the secular. If you take a close look at the lifestyle of Hebrew believers you will find that their faith and their work are seamlessly integrated. God ingrained His faith-life-work ethic into Jewish culture and it remains strong to this day. When I was in football, I was a Christian. And when I was pastoring and preaching, I was a Christian! I never thought of the two aspects as distinct from one another. If any footballer I worked with in the past walked into my church this Sunday, I would have nothing to hide. I wouldn't be worried about the way I had behaved in the past, the conversations I'd had, or the inappropriate jokes I'd told.

I believe it was because my work was worship unto God that I was so successful in business. I wouldn't attribute it to anything else. That's how a man who couldn't read or write before the age of eighteen became one of the top 300 life insurance salesmen in the world. My utmost concern was that I honoured

God. Consequently I gave less time to the job than other salesmen did, and yet I was more effective. I could do more business in one week than many other men could do in a month. There are so many books on management available in our bookstores, and yet the Bible contains life-changing, working principles that outdo them all!

Our worships leads us to a revelation of God's glory

As we worship God we get to know more of Him. It's a very simple principle and process. The more we open ourselves up to God and surrender to Him in worship, the more God reveals Himself to us, and at the same time hears our prayers and meets our needs. It is impossible to live a life committed to worshipping of God and not eventually experience His glory. And our experience of Him is so different from that of our predecessors.

In the Old Testament people would come and bring their sacrifices and offerings to the temple in order to "connect" with God and have their sins forgiven. But they could only get as far as the outer door of the temple. From there on it was the task of the priests to prepare and offer the sacrifices. And it was only the High Priest, and then only once a year, who was able to go through the veil and enter in to the Holy of Holies where the ark of the covenant lay covered by the mercy seat – the place where the very presence of God dwelt.

The mercy seat, positioned as it was directly over the ark of the covenant containing the law, was a vivid and powerful picture of what Christ would do, and has done, for us. The law brought judgement and death, but we are saved by God's overriding mercy through Christ. Jesus' blood provided the ultimate sacrifice for us. During the temple sacrifices hundreds of lambs and young bulls were slain as sin offerings, but the atonement for all our sins for all time was encompassed in Christ's sacrifice on the cross.

When Solomon built his temple, he realised that wherever God's glory was, there the angelic hosts would also be in attendance. It is fascinating to me that any church that experiences a glimpse of revival will often become aware of the presence of angels. Where the glory of God is manifest, and where Jesus is truly worshipped, angels gather. Angels are, in essence, the protectors of God's glory. There are several instances in the Bible – such as the angel who was set on guard outside the garden of Eden, and the angel who confronted Balaam with a sword – where angels have been commissioned to ensure the glory of God is not violated.

Years ago in Durban, South Africa, I had a remarkable experience of the glory of God and angelic visitation. I was preaching in a church there and having finished my sermon was calling people out to respond to the message. Later a very respectable doctor came to speak to me and told me of the astonishing sight he had witnessed as I prayed for the people. He told me that standing behind me was a very tall angel. He turned to look at the back of the room and there he saw a second enormous angel. When I spoke the name of Jesus in my praying, the two angels bowed towards one another, and such was the span of their great wings that the tips touched. It reminded me of the two gigantic cherubim that Solomon fashioned for his temple with their wings touching. The doctor said that at the precise moment when the angel's wings touched, the power of God fell on the gathered people and everyone fell under the power of the Holy Spirit.

Even now it stirs deep emotions inside me to recall this event. As I was thinking about it again recently, God spoke to me and said, "David, in Durban you were in a holy place. Those angels were in your meeting because you had come to the mercy seat of Christ, sprinkled by His blood. They 'covered' that meeting because you had entered into the Holy of Holies." Sadly, the Church rarely seems to go there today, and yet what better place could there be for us than dwelling in the glory of God's presence? No wonder that on that day in Durban people fell under God's power; no wonder they were healed and saved. God had visited them in their affliction. I want to belong to a church like that!

Since Christ's great sacrifice for us, the whole nature of our interaction with God has changed radically. Jesus came, not to make the law redundant, but to fulfil it completely. As our perfect High Priest He has removed the veil that separated us from God's holy presence and we can freely enter in because of His blood. All true believers are welcomed into the Most Holy Place, yet many prefer to stay behind in the outer courts, on the periphery of God's presence. Why is that?

We must be a worshipping church! A church where the presence of God comes amongst us regardless of the style of music or the structure of the service. More than that, whether it's at church on Sunday, or at the office on Monday; in the factories, hospitals, or stuck in traffic jams, we must be a worshipping people who live in God's presence!

Worship is never about music but lifestyle. I challenge everyone to join me in the dedication of our lives to be worshippers: to worship the Lord in the beauty of His holiness; to worship the Lord and bow down; to worship the Lord and kiss Him; worship the Lord at the mercy seat. May you worship God in your living, in your giving, in your worship, in your singing, in your dancing; may you worship Him in your home, in your workplace, in your marriage, in your singleness, may you worship God always. Amen.

Worship – Part 2

Christians are often guilty of being conservative in their efforts to read the Bible. People tend to read the little bits of Scripture that appeal to them, but are often unaware of the context surrounding their favourite verses. This is true of the often quoted Psalm 100. We know well verse 4 that says,

> *"Enter into His gates with thanksgiving,*
> *And into His courts with praise.*
> *Be thankful to Him, and bless His name."*

But focusing only on this statement can cause us to miss something vital. There are a number of conditions to be met *before* we enter into God's presence with thanksgiving and praise as we will see.

David, the writer of this psalm, lived in an age where there did not exist the freedom of expression in worship that the modern Church enjoys. Yet his worship to God was exuberant and sacrificial. David knew what it meant to *really* worship God. He even danced before the Lord in his underwear, despite what anyone else might think of him! He had a depth of expression to his worship that many believers today don't possess, even after the revelation of the cross and the gift of the Holy Spirit. We have more revelation than David ever had; we have more of the Holy Spirit than David ever experienced; and yet David puts most of us to shame with his passion for God.

I see in this psalm a picture of what our devotional life should look like when it comes to worshipping God. David was determined every Sabbath to, "enter His gates with thanksgiving and His courts with praise." He had decided that his lifestyle would be one of thankfulness to God and of continually blessing Him. This should give us pause for thought. What is our devotional worship life like? How disciplined are we at turning up each week to "enter His gates" and worship God? We can't just turn up when we feel like it, when we can find the space in our diary, or when things are going well. The Sabbath day – Sunday as it is in the West – is all about God, not about us. It is primarily about us blessing God, and not God blessing us!

> **"Anyone can be a 'top coat' Christian, wearing a thin layer of gloss that looks good from a distance – but do we stand up to closer inspection?"**

People tell me, since I'm not a great DIY enthusiast, that the key to doing a good job is *preparation*. The quality of the preparation will determine the success, or failure, of the finished product. If you are restoring a car's bodywork then it is the painstaking sanding down, filling in, rubbing down etc., that determines how good the car looks once it is sprayed. When that final layer of gloss goes on, the finish will only be flawless if sufficient effort has gone into the preparation.

Anyone can be a "top coat" Christian, wearing a thin layer of gloss that looks good from a distance – but do we stand up to closer inspection? Anyone can throw a few impressive Bible verses around and pass themselves off as spiritual – until they encounter some real hardship. As a preacher who always used to be pressed for time, I could stand up and preach a message off the top of my head. But the trouble with that was people only ever got a "top of their head" blessing! I did this until I took seriously Paul's admonition to his protégé Timothy to "study to be approved" as a man capable of handling God's Word.

It is a fact in any sphere of life that you get out of something what you put into it. If you put minimal effort into your relationships, then you will get a minimal return. If you are shallow, you'll only get your feet wet! So what preparations should we make before we enter into God's presence to worship Him? What things must happen before we pass through those gates? Before I list three things that the psalmist says are important, let us note that it is *we* who have some work to do before we turn up to church on a Sunday. It is not down to the worship leader and his team to get us motivated and enthusiastically worshipping God. Our "worship experience" should not be based on how good the worship team is, but on how good we are! I can sing the old hymns with tears running down my face and I can jump up and down to the latest up-tempo modern choruses – it doesn't make any difference to me as long as the music is glorifying to God. But if I have a miserable, critical attitude, I will wipe out the value of either!

Shout to the Lord

The first precondition for entering God's gates with thanksgiving is found in verse 1 of Psalm 100:

"Make a joyful shout to the LORD."

The first thing we need to do if we are going to be authentic worshippers is to clear our lungs! When my granddaughter Poppy was born, as with all new babies, the medical staff had to ensure that all the mucus was cleared out of her lungs so that she was able to breathe properly. You know for sure when this has happened when you hear the baby crying for the first time. In fact, the very first cry a baby utters is actually helping that process of clearing the lungs. Similarly, before we come to God expecting to enter into worship, we should have declared a shout of joy to the Lord to begin to prepare our hearts. Wouldn't it be wonderful if, instead of being disturbed by the sound of your TV or radio late at night, your neighbours were awakened at 7.00am on a Sunday morning by a shout of *"Praise Be to God!"* I'd much rather be evicted for being zealous for God than being a nuisance!

Serve the Lord with gladness

The next precondition is in the first half of verse 2 of Psalm 100:

"Serve the LORD with gladness."

Again we see the Bible telling us that our service is worship to God, just as we saw that our work is worship in the previous chapter. What does it mean to serve the Lord with gladness? Do we say to ourselves, "Oh no, I'm meant to be on car park duty this week. I think I'll tell them I'm ill"? Whatever your sphere of service, that kind of attitude isn't going to help you to be a worshipper. There are people at our church who help with the TV broadcasts of our services who quietly work away in the background all the time and whose names don't even appear on the credits at the end of the programme. People who attend our services wouldn't particularly notice what they were doing, yet they are serving the Lord with gladness. It is part of their worship to the Lord.

If part of your involvement at your local church means you turn up early to hump equipment about, or perhaps you are a steward on the door who greets people, both those tasks are a precursor to your worship. They are acts of service that should be carried out with gladness, not moaning. Please, never go around muttering, "Nobody appreciates me." You are not there for people to appreciate you – you're there for God to appreciate you, and He does! The Bible says that which is done in private will be made public, so continue serving the Lord with gladness and He will reward you.

Come before His presence with singing

The second half of Psalm 100:2 says,

"Come before His presence with singing."

Whenever someone's football team wins the cup, the fans are dancing in the streets in celebration. It's easy to sing when you're winning and be carried along with the euphoria of the moment, but a real supporter sings even when their team is losing. Similarly, anyone is liable to praise God when they are feeling on top form; anyone can wear the team shirt when their church is thriving, all the services are packed and the atmosphere is buzzing. But do you worship God with the same enthusiasm when you've just received bad news? When you've just found out you are being made redundant, or when you're feeling depressed? Are you still committed to come before God's presence with singing then?

Singing out our praise to God when we least feel like it can be a very powerful weapon in the believer's armoury. Not singing God's praises because, "we don't feel like it" is often the very cause of the mess we are in! Praise actually has nothing to do with feelings. David insisted that we should worship the Lord and sing His praises *despite* our circumstances. This precondition also shows us the importance of engaging in worshipping God privately before coming together with other believers to worship God publicly and corporately. If we are not worshippers when we are on our own, then we will find it hard to "warm up" and worship God sincerely when we gather as a church.

Know that the Lord is God

Lastly, David says in verse 3,

> *"Know that the LORD, He is God."*

Incredibly, all these things should be in place in our lives before we think about coming to worship God. Everything we have looked at so far can be called "outside church" stuff that should make up the fabric of our everyday lives. David realised this and acted on it. In the latter part of verse 3 he also gives us three reasons why he did so – and we have all the more reason to do so!

1. *"...He is God."* We worship God because of who He is. We live in the revelation of the Lordship of Christ. We know who Jesus our Saviour is. We worship Him not because we *think* He is God, but because we *know* He is God. We know that Jesus our redeemer lives. We are confident of who

Jesus is because we have a far greater revelation through Scripture regarding His identity than David ever did.

2. *"It is He who has made us, and not we ourselves..."* We live in the knowledge that God is our creator. We have been made by Him. We have not evolved; we are not self-created. It is a wonderful thing to know where you came from. That alone should give us the motivation we need to go to church on Sunday and worship God! We know not only that we were created by God, but also that He made us for a specific purpose. God has a specific, unique plan for your life. Even if you were an orphan or came into the world in the most terrible of circumstances, God planned your life with a purpose in mind. God knew you and loved you before the foundation of the world. Doesn't that make you want to praise Him?

3. *"We are His people and the sheep of His pasture."* Not only is He our God, but we are His people. If God was only our God, then it would be a somewhat one-sided arrangement; we would not be much better off than the superstitious tribes-people worshipping a fearsome and vengeful god that you see in old movies. But God has said to us, "You are My people." Through Christ He has established a two-way relationship with us. In Great Britain, Elizabeth is our Queen, and technically, we are her people, her subjects. Very few of us are actually on speaking terms with her though! We don't know her directly. Amazingly, the God of the universe has decreed

that we should know Him directly and has made a way for that to happen through His Son. He is our God, we are His people, and we can meet with Him every day!

There is so much we need to grasp about our relationship with the Father and the way in which we relate to Him, and so much we need to include in our lifestyle – and we haven't even arrived at the place of worship yet! If we came to God's courts with this understanding, with these biblical disciplines in our lives, we would be on fire before we even got through the door! All we would need the worship band to do is fan the flame!

Now and now only does the psalmist say,

> *"Enter into His gates with thanksgiving,*
> *And into His courts with praise.*
> *Be thankful to Him, and bless His name."*

When we come to church already a worshipping person, we will have a very different perspective on our Sunday service. We need to understand that revival churches are more interested in "worship" than merely "singing".

Forget not all His benefits

One admonition that appears many times in Scripture is the command to "forget not all His benefits". Psalm

103:2 is one of the verses that mentions this, but Psalm 103 also goes on to list what they are. The psalmist reminds us that we have so much to be thankful to God for and so much encouragement to live a life of worship to Him. God, the psalmist says, is the One who...

1. "... forgives all your iniquities" (v. 3)

If you truly believe that God has forgiven all your sins, then when you come to worship Him there should be a freedom in your soul. The number of Christians who are weighed down by the guilt of past sins is really alarming! But the psalmist insists that the reason he worships God is because He has forgiven all his sins. We need to live in the place of repentance and keep short accounts with God and one another so that we don't spend our lives carrying around unnecessary baggage. If you slip up, repent and say sorry to God and then receive His forgiveness. Also ask Him to cleanse and restore you so that you don't then carry any guilt or shame around with you.

2. "... who heals all your diseases" (v. 3)

With all my heart I believe that God is committed to healing us and to me that is a great reason to praise Him. Although it is not widespread in our nation at the moment, God has done some amazing miracles in our midst. At our church we have seen numbers of people healed of cancer. If we don't get incredibly excited about that and jump up and down, then with respect, we should be ashamed of ourselves. We jump for joy every time someone whose life was going to be tragically cut short is healed and does not die prematurely.

3. "...who redeems your life from destruction" (v. 4)
Jesus has redeemed us from destruction. In other words, He has literally "bought" us back. But God the Father is also committed to redeeming us from the dangers inherent in everyday life, just as He "redeemed" me from the potentially fatal car accident I mentioned in the previous chapter. Later I asked the Lord why I had been a target of the enemy and He told me it was because I had been teaching on the subject of angels. I like to raise people's awareness of the angelic host that surrounds us on a daily basis and to take people's focus off the demonic. I believe it is part of the enemy's strategy to have us talking about demons all the time. In reality, those who are with us and far more than those who are against us! After we realise that God is able to save us from injury or even death, then we can no longer sit and sulk in our Sunday services because they are not quite to our liking!

4. "...who crowns you with lovingkindness and tender mercies" (v. 4)
God is continually showing His love to us and pouring out His mercy upon us. What love the Father has bestowed upon us that we may be called the sons of God. Not just love, but kindness joined together, not just mercy but tender mercy, typical of God – excessive in His blessings towards His children. Through the crown He exalts us to high planes, the crown confirms

office, authority, position – we are special people – praise His name.

5. *"... who satisfies your mouth with good things"* (v. 5)
Some people never seem to be satisfied with church no matter what is on offer. Some only like the old hymns, some only the new choruses; some people are not fond of the worship at all and only come for the Bible teaching! The fact is, we don't need any more, better, or different things to enhance our church life because we haven't even absorbed what we've got! If we thoroughly applied even a fraction of what we know, we would be transformed people!

6. *"... who renews our youth like the eagle"* (v. 5)
One of the miracles of the spiritual life is that God has the ability to renew our strength as we continue to wait on and abide in Him. He is able to revitalise and reenergise us. Sometimes it amazes me how God can do that. You just have to thank Him for it.

> **"It is a good discipline to take time to look back and reflect on what God has done for you. In looking back you realise just how much blessing there has been."**

Recently I had two unexpected reunions. First of all I met with a very old friend with whom I had worked closely more than thirty-seven years ago when we were both bouncers. Over the years we had lost touch, but he found me on the internet and got in contact. John had been my best friend all those years ago. We found ourselves in some very tight spots at times and we learned to watch one another's back. You bond with someone very quickly when you have to fight side by side and look out for each other. So it was that a short while later I found myself visiting him in his home. Sadly John had experienced some hard times in life and things were tough. Years earlier he had been involved in a car accident and had walked away apparently unscathed, but later when he began to have intermittent blackouts, his doctors discovered the accident had left scarring on his brain. As a result he had lost his driving licence and he was continually so drugged up that he was beginning to lose his memory. On top of this he had recently been diagnosed with cancer.

My heart went out to my old friend. In addition to all his personal health problems, there were a number of difficult issues to cope with in his wider family. After our visit, Molly and I got into our car and I literally wept. "Look how good God has been to us," I said. As believers, sometimes we forget how much God has done for us. As well as the amazing privilege of being redeemed by Christ, God blesses us in so many ways. He renews our strength!

The second reunion was a gathering of all the people who used to belong to our youth group when we were teenagers. Again, this gave us pause for thought. There were some who didn't turn up at all because they were backslidden believers. Others had been through difficult marriages and had divorced. Others were broken and depressed. Molly and I left this reunion once again rehearsing God's goodness to us and "forgetting not all His benefits."

It is a good discipline to take time to look back and reflect on what God has done for you. In looking back you realise just how much blessing there has been. Everyone we met at our reunion was tired or burnt out and we thanked God that we were not.

What does it mean to have your strength renewed like that of an eagles? The eagle is the king of all birds and yet he makes himself vulnerable doing something that no other bird does. Every few years, when the eagle realises that the heights he can soar to are no longer as high as they once were, he retreats to his nest and voluntarily plucks out his flight feathers. It means that he can't fly any more! For a time he makes himself incredibly vulnerable, but he stays in the nest until new flight feathers grow. When the new feathers appear, the eagle can soar to his former heights and is like a young eagle again.

What does this mean for us? It means we have to be that vulnerable before God if we want to continually be renewed by Him. We must, at times, allow God to hem us in so that He takes away our means of escape. Then, after He deals with us, we are renewed in our strength and capable of soaring to previously unattainable heights.

7. "...who executes righteousness and justice for all who are oppressed" (v. 6)
We worship God because He cares about us when we are stressed and pressured. God is the champion of all

who are oppressed and He longs to act on our behalf. When we suffer injustice, God notices and determines to do something about it. Our problem is that we rarely appreciate God's timetable for righting wrongs. We like to take the law into our own hands and execute what we believe to be "justice" whenever we are treated badly. Why is it that we always take it upon ourselves to bring judgement on those who hurt us when the Lord says, "Vengeance is mine"? More than thirty years ago an incident occurred that could easily have wrecked my life. I was deeply wounded by the actions of another person and I could have lived in unforgiveness for the rest of my life. I had a choice to make. Thank God I made the right one. I am where I am today because I made a decision to forgive that person on the spot. Forgiveness, like worship, is an act of the will.

When we meet together

My desire for our church is for us to become a people of sacred adoration – a people who will bring to the house of God a lifestyle so full of thankfulness and adoration that it sweeps through the church at every level. In Philippians 3:3 Paul speaks about "true circumcision" – the circumcision of the heart, rather than the flesh. He is referring to the fact that in Christ our human spirit has been separated from our carnal nature. We are ones who, Paul says, "worship God in the Spirit." In other words, we don't have to come to church dominated by all of our carnal desires – we can come and worship God in the power of the Holy Spirit. We have no confidence in the flesh, but we rely on the Spirit to help us.

> **"You need other believers around you to build you up and for you to build them up. In order to have your faith enlarged like that, you have to be in the house of God."**

Hebrews 10:25 is a verse that is often quoted when we think about the issue of God's people meeting together:

> *"... not forsaking the assembling of ourselves together, as is the manner of some, but exhorting one another, and so much the more as you see the Day approaching."*

Often this verse has been used to encourage people to attend church regularly, to not "forsake meeting together", but I believe the key phrase in this verse is "exhorting one another". It is not just the fact of meeting together that is important, but that we exhort one another. It means to build one another up. It is simply not possible to do that on your own! You need other believers around you to build you up and for you to build them up. In order to have your faith enlarged like that, you have to be in the house of God.

The restoration of the family altar

Recently, our worship leader Tim Uluirewa said something at a minister's fraternal which set me thinking. He was speaking about the expectation he had that every member of his worship team would be an authentic worshipper – people who worship God off the platform as well as on it. He went a step further by suggesting there is a need for the head of every household to instigate times of family worship, where the family unit gathers to worship God together on a regular basis. In years gone by, Pentecostal colleagues of mine would refer to this as the "family altar". The truth is, few Charismatic believers today practise the discipline of holding family worship times – to our shame.

Tim's comments set me on a journey to look at the importance placed upon family worship in Jewish tradition. The concept of "family" has always been central in God's nature, His thinking and in His guidance of us. Modern society has done much to damage and fracture the family unit and the boundaries of the "normal" family are constantly being breeched. But Jewish tradition has sought to protect the sanctity of the family. Whilst we must take care to note that the following "rituals" belong to people who don't necessarily know Jesus and are still trying to live under the law, there are many useful principles to be gleaned.

The father or mother of a Jewish family leads Friday worship, called the *Shabbat* – the equivalent to our

Sunday in the West. It is the day of rest and lasts from before sunset on Friday until nightfall on Saturday. The purpose of the day is to celebrate and honour God and to remember the day of rest that He initiated after creation.

Under Jewish law there are thirty-nine things you are not allowed to do on the Sabbath. Jews see it primarily as a time for spiritual growth and of focusing on family and community involvement. The restrictions are therefore largely to do with not working. On the Friday the father of the family goes to the synagogue and has a time of greeting for the Sabbath. There are particular prayers and six psalms are recited which represent the six working days. Then a number of benedictions are given which focus mainly on the following issues:

- Acknowledging the mightiness of God in nature
- Prayers for sanctification
- Prayers for understanding and for penitence
- Prayers for forgiveness, redemption, healing
- Thanks for the blessings of the harvest
- The reward of the righteous
- Praise and thanksgiving
- The restoration of the kingdom of David and the temple

On his arrival back home, the father blesses his children and recites another benediction. The father will hold his sons in his arms and pronounce over them, "May God make you like Ephraim and Mannasseh. For the girls he says, "May God make you as Sarah, Rebbecah, Rachel and Leah." Then he calls all of them together and says, "May God bless you and guard you. May the light of God shine upon you and may God be gracious to you. May the presence of God be with you and give you His peace."

Also (although it is not done so often nowadays because of the women's liberation movement), an orthodox Jew will sometimes turn to his wife and sing to her the verses of Proverbs 31:1-31, extolling her virtues and declaring his love and appreciation for her. Ladies, imagine if your husband did that for you every single Friday!

The father will then have a full cup of wine which symbolizes the overflowing of joy and bounty and both physical and spiritual completion; and he will eat two braided pieces of bread which speak of the extra manna that was provided for the day of rest. The rest of the night is spent in the study of the Torah or talking to family and friends who are in the house.

> **"Men, as the God-appointed head of their family, should be the ones who initiate times of family worship."**

Whilst clearly I am not suggesting that we should all embark on a similar ritual observance ourselves, you can see amidst this powerful imagery the richness that such a regular time of worship and remembrance brings to life. Men, as the God-appointed head of their family, should be the ones who initiate these times of family worship. At the time of the Passover in Egypt, it was the father's responsibility to gather his family into the house and cover it with the blood when the angel of death flew over the land. Similarly, worship for us all, Jew or Gentile, is inextricably interwoven between our personal faith, our family faith and our corporate faith. It is a lifestyle of praise and homage.

It is interesting that the Jews, the Muslims, the Hindus and the Sikhs, all adhere to a set time of worship both in their homes, their work, and at church. Among Christians it is only the Orthodox Church that has a lifestyle of prescribed worship. Evangelicals and Pentecostals – more so among those who have a "free church" mentality – have largely discarded any form of formal worship as legalism contending that it belongs to the "Old Covenant". And yet, without having any set time of worship in the home, they expect their church's children's ministry to bring their kids up for them and turn them into worshippers!

I believe you can remain true to tradition and still enjoy freedom. For the last 800 years every day, 365 days per year, without fail, in St Alphege Church in Solihull, they have worshipped God and prayed for the town. Every day at the same time for 800 years! You may well ask, have those prayers always been delivered by Bible believing clergy? Have they all meant what they prayed? That's a good question and the answer is, probably not. However, that is not the fault of the structure. The structure makes time to pray every day. Similarly, we need to see the "family altar" restored in our generation, because when we make time for God, He makes time for us. No wonder so many people struggle with hearing God's voice. If we make space for regular times of worship and prayer during our home life, I suspect we will all begin to hear Him much better!

Don't let business steal your special day with God

When I was in business I was the only Gentile amongst a number of Jews. If you want to know how to live out your faith in your daily life, then watch the Jews – or the Muslims for that matter! These men were highly successful in business, but they never compromised the Sabbath or time with their families. They liked me because I always respected and observed the Lord's day. "Many Christians," they would tell me, "compromise their faith to suit their business life."

I was also careful to conduct myself in a godly way whenever I had to work away from home or was attending a conference. Usually at these events there was some kind of "entertainment" on offer in the evenings. Sometimes it was a show, other times a nightclub. For those who didn't want to be part of that scene, there would be a less racy alternative. On one such occasion the "alternative" was a meal at a lovely restaurant. I made my choice and walked into the restaurant looking for any colleagues that might also be there. Sure enough there was a Jewish colleague and his wife. He said to me, "I knew you'd be here because you're different from the other Christians we know. I knew you wouldn't want to go to any of those places."

The same man told me that he never did business on a Friday or a Saturday. "What I do," he explained, "is lock myself away with my wife and kids and we celebrate the Shabbat, then we go to the synagogue. That never alters." He asked me, "What do you do?" I told him that I never worked on a Sunday unless I was on duty as an emergency call out.

If you are a doctor, a nurse, a bus driver on shifts, or something similar then I believe it's different for you. But when you are in control of your destiny on a weekend you should observe the Lord's day. A good Jew will never work on the Sabbath and a good Christian does not work on the Lord's day because it's his/her worship day! It's not about legalism. If you are not forced to work on a Sunday, then don't. People have said to me in the past, "If I work on a Sunday I get double time." The Lord help you! If you can't run your finances based on six days per week, then you should quit working altogether!

All throughout my business life God has been faithful to me as I took care to protect my day of worship. My colleagues would be incredulous that I would turn business away rather than work on a Sunday, but I would always say to them, "If I turn down a £20,000 deal on Sunday because it's the Lord's day, a few days later He will give me a £40,000 deal!" God is no man's debtor. Baron John Laing who was the head of one of the largest building companies in the UK was a Christian and never worked on a Sunday. He was always found at the communion table every Sunday and God made him hugely successful.

Tithing our time

The Bible calls worship our "reasonable service". It is something we are duty bound to perform. However, we don't worship God because He demands it from us, we worship Him because of His amazing grace and mercy towards us. When we speak of tithing to God, we do a disservice to the biblical principle when we think of it only in terms of cash. Our tithing to God also needs to include our time. There are 168 hours in one week.

> "In our busy society, we are not overworked,
> we are under-worshipped! God wants us to be
> successful people and to prosper us in our work,
> but when we allow the success and the
> prosperity to dominate our thinking
> we have fallen into idolatry."

If we gave the Lord just ten percent of our time then it would be just short of seventeen hours. How many of us give God even that amount of time in a normal week? A recent poll revealed that we spend more time than that each week watching the TV (nineteen hours per week in the US and eighteen hours per week in the UK)! If we spend half an hour reading our Bible each morning, half and hour praying each evening, and go to church every Sunday, we will still have given God less than ten hours of our time. It doesn't sound like a lot does it? The fact is, in our busy society, we are not overworked, we are under-worshipped! God wants us to be successful people and to prosper us in our work, but when we allow the success and the prosperity to dominate our thinking we have fallen into idolatry.

I want to close this section by recalling an incredibly vivid dream I had just before the Lord called me to be a pastor. The dream was so real it was almost tangible. In the dream I was dying. I was lying on a hospital bed, surrounded by doctors who were talking over me, commenting to each other that I was slipping away fast. I began to panic and I called out, "Isn't there anything you can do?"

One of the doctors spoke to me and said, "Well, you won't be needing your car now..."

"You can have it!" I said. "The keys are over there."

"You won't be needing your house either," the doctor said.

"You can have my house too," I said. "Just don't let me die."

The doctor took an inventory of my whole life. He spoke about everything: my wife, my kids, my clothes. I was willing to give them all up if he would just let me live. Then suddenly the room went dark and a bright light came into the room. A voice said, "You can live." Just then an overwhelming sense of joy washed over me. I was able to get off the bed and stand up. I knew I wasn't going to die. I found myself face to face with the doctor once again and he said to me, "You can go now."

"But, I've got nothing now," I said. "I've got no clothes, no car to drive away in, no house, no family. Nothing."

The doctor put his hand in his pocket and pulled out a bunch of keys. "Here," he said. "Drive my car." The keys were the same ones I had given him earlier. "It's not your car any more, it's mine, but I am going to let you drive it." Then he said to me, "Here are the keys to *my* house. You can live there rent free. And by the way, the wife and kids you gave me will be waiting for you when you get back. The job you gave up is still there for you. But from now on remember, they are mine and I can have them back at any time."

The day after that dream God called me to give up my well paid job to be a pastor. If I had failed to respond to the dream God initiated, I would not be doing what I'm doing today.

Worship is our work, our play, our family, our life. It is very little to do with the songs we sing in church and everything to do with the expression of our souls to our Creator. I believe the degree to which we make worship central to our lives will determine the degree to which we are blessed and fulfilled in Christ. The Bible says we should, "Bless the Lord at all times" and let His praise be "continually" in our mouths. Obeying that command is of primary importance in any church that seeks to live in revival.

Word – Part 1

Some time ago a very bleak report came across my desk that explained the findings of some research carried out among all the church denominations in the UK and Ireland. The report suggested that the number of people attending church in our nation is continually diminishing. I was invited onto a radio programme to discuss the report and during the debate I made the following point: we are very likely to see the numbers in our congregations dwindle if the clergy persists in explaining away much of our Christian faith. I believe people actually want to hear the truth of the Bible, not some insipid, watered down gospel made to be "acceptable" in modern society.

Responses to the report were numerous and colourful. Here are what some other ministers had to say:

> "Tinkering around with service times or liturgy won't work if the message isn't there. The heart of the matter is, congregations want to hear what the Bible says in a relevant way with conviction and passion."

> "It is a myth to say that the people of this country have rejected Christianity. They simply haven't been told enough about it to either accept or reject it."

Thousands of letters, however, took a similar line to this poor person:

> "We used to go to church expecting very little and came away with nothing. This has now changed to expecting nothing and coming away with even less. What we want are services taken with conviction and with the passion of Christ."

A member of the Anglican Deanery Synod of Whitby said, "It is obvious moral values have deteriorated over the past fifty years, but some churches seem to do little or nothing about it and remain silent. Church ministers must not become tolerant of such things but condemn sin, whilst at the same time, loving the sinner. Ministers who do this will find their congregation swelling."

"Without the message of the cross, Christianity is only a good idea, another set of religious beliefs or a high moral code."

It seems to me that preaching the message of the cross is deemed to be of very little value today in many churches. But without that teaching, the masses may rightly ask the question: "What has God ever done for me?" Without the message of the cross, Christianity is only a good idea, another set of religious beliefs or a high moral code. Without the power of the cross a person can go through life and claim, "Believing in God hasn't done anything for me. It hasn't helped my failing marriage; it hasn't improved my health." But when you realise that Christ has taken all your sin to the cross, confronted and defeated death on your behalf; when you see that the cross is now empty and Christ is risen – that He can heal your body and your marriage, that He can help you run your business and live your life successfully – then everything is different. Unless you preach the cross, Jesus has done nothing – but He has in fact done everything! Why do so many ministers avoid preaching this?

The final conclusion of the report was this: "It is only since the film *The Passion of the Christ* that many people have started to understand what Jesus did." It's sad that it takes a film to reach people with a message that has been plainly available in print for centuries. We must rekindle our passion for preaching the message of the Bible with passion and authority. Although worship is vitally important, we must recapture an awesome respect for the Word.

In the beginning was the Word

One of the most amazing statements about Jesus in the entire Bible is found in the first chapter of John's gospel. There we read,

> *"In the beginning was the Word, and the Word was with God, and the Word was God. He was in the beginning with God."*
>
> (John 1:1–2)

It blows my mind to read that Jesus is described as "the Word". At this stage "the Word" wasn't something that was written down – it was a Person! The written Word came later. John goes on to say,

> *"All things were made through Him, and without Him nothing was made that was made. In Him was life, and the life was the light of men. And the light shines in the darkness, and the darkness did not comprehend it."*
>
> (John 1:3–5)

Later in verse 14 John makes the amazing statement that the *"Word became flesh and dwelt among us."* This "living Word" – Jesus – caused the written Word, the Bible, to come into being. The Old Testament is packed full of prophecies and foreshadowings of His arrival on earth and His eventual appearance spawned all the writings of the New Testament. The Word we read today came out of the Word who became flesh. It is literally the "diary of God" and includes His thoughts, His teachings, and the revelations He desires to share with His creation mankind. Importantly it also contains His commandments to us so that we can enjoy a fruitful and satisfying life on earth and beyond into eternity.

Speaking of God's commands, a young man recently got confirmed in the Anglican church and on the way out of the service another Christian commented to him, "So what do you think of the Ten Commandments?" The young man said, "The Ten what?" He didn't know what they were! Why is this so? It can only be for a

lack of reading the Bible and a lack of exposure to true
biblical preaching.

The Bible gets me incredibly excited. The words
contained in it are the divinely transcribed writings
of anointed men direct from the heart of God. It is a
collection of love letters, poetry, songs and historical
records. I get excited because in the beginning the
Word – the *logos* – was there with God. He existed.
The Bible says that all things were made through
Him. In Him was life! This is still true today: there is
life in the Word of God! If we don't preach the Word
then the life won't get released and change people's
lives.

John described Jesus as the *"light of men"* and said
that, *"the light shines in the darkness, and the darkness
did not comprehend it"* (John 1:4–5). Darkness will
always shrink from the light. Later in his first epistle,
the apostle wrote this:

> *"That which was from the beginning, which we
> have heard, which we have seen with our eyes,
> which we have looked upon, and our hands have
> handled, concerning the Word of life – the life was
> manifested, and we have seen, and bear witness,
> and declare to you that eternal life which was with
> the Father and was manifested to us – that which
> we have seen and heard we declare to you, that
> you also may have fellowship with us; and truly
> our fellowship is with the Father and with His Son
> Jesus Christ. And these things we write to you that
> your joy may be full."*

> (1 John 1:1–4)

Notice in these incredible verses how John speaks about the incarnate Word of God – the Word relates to our senses – hearing, seeing, touching ... and elsewhere the Bible says taste and see that the Lord is good. The Word is not some dry, ancient piece of parchment containing words that are irrelevant to us in the modern world. No! It is alive and active and is capable not only of reaching our mind, but interacting with all our senses and piercing our very souls as well.

The power of the Word

In the light of this it is amazing to me that so many ministers – who are after all stewards of the Word of God – try to minimise the impact of certain truths it contains. During the same radio interview I mentioned earlier the interviewer asked one of the other guests, a theologian, "How will you celebrate Easter today in your Baptist church?" He replied saying that they would be celebrating the resurrection, but then cast some doubt on whether the resurrection really took place as Scripture tells it. Challenging him on this point I asked why he wasn't sure about it, to which he replied, "Well, the Bible is very confusing. One person said they saw Jesus on the road, others saw Him when He cooked breakfast for them. There are so many opinions."

Sometimes I wonder if life isn't simpler when you are thick! Some theologians think too much! I mentioned the car accident that I described in an earlier section of this book to my theologian friend. "One witness may have seen that girl's car spin around," I said. "Someone else may have seen the car career over the hill. Each witness had their own version of the story to tell, but it doesn't alter the fact that the girl had a car accident. All the witnesses provide the evidence that it actually happened. In the same way, the people who saw Jesus on the road and the people who saw Him cooking breakfast are providing us with the evidence that He did indeed rise from the dead!"

> **"The reason why many people don't want to get too deep into the Word of God is because it is so convicting, so confrontational, so life-changing."**

The book of Hebrews gives us another vivid description of the power of the Word:

> *"For the word of God is living and powerful, and sharper than any two-edged sword, piercing even to the division of soul and spirit, and of joints and marrow, and is a discerner of the thoughts and intents of the heart."*
>
> (Hebrews 4:12)

The Word of God is "living and powerful", not dead on the cross or lying in a grave! I think the reason why many people don't want to get too deep into the Word of God is because it is so convicting, so confrontational, so life-changing. The Bible can change the way you think, change the way you act, change the way you live. If we don't read the Bible then we can stay in our comfort zones. Ignorance is bliss, we think. No, ignorance is sin.

Jesus came to earth as the Living Word and left a legacy of the Word so that we might understand God's heart and be transformed. The writer of Hebrews points out that the Word has the ability to "pierce" soul and spirit. Scripture is so powerful it has the ability to separate man's thoughts, intents and actions. It is a powerful instrument of divine diagnostic. It helps us to understand that God knows exactly where we are at, what's wrong with us, and what needs to happen in order for Him to cure us.

The Bible reveals the nature of God to man and in so doing helps us to realise the dilemma of humankind. When we read the Bible it is like reading a letter sent directly from God to us. It is as if the Word says, "Dear David, I want you to look at yourself in the light of looking at Me. Look at Me and look at yourself. Look at yourself and look at Me." That's how the Bible works. It is as simple as that. The Bible is the mirror of the soul.

God's Word is the record of all the thoughts, commands, revelations and prophetic utterances that flow from the throne of God. God visited different ones of His servants and inspired them to write His words down under the flow of the Holy Spirit. The Bible is a book that interprets and explains itself and so we read in 2 Timothy 3:16 that,

"All Scripture is given by inspiration of God, and is profitable for doctrine, for reproof, for correction, for instruction in righteousness."

What this tells us is that if we will faithfully preach the Word and accept its correction and instruction it will produce a profit in our lives. We will be in credit! When you read the Bible you are never poorer for doing so, but richer. When you base your life on the Word of God you are never destitute, you are in supply. That is why I am so committed to preaching God's Word to people. In our church we don't have ten minute sermons. If you preach sermonettes then you produce Christianettes! Instead we want to get deep into God's Word and let its power impact our lives.

When Jesus was tempted by the devil in the wilderness He relied on the power of the Word alone to overcome His trial. He didn't say to the enemy, "What you've said is quite interesting, let's debate that for a while." Jesus simply said, "It is written . . . " When the devil said, "You're hungry, turn these stones into bread," Jesus said, "It is written, man shall not live by bread alone . . . " When the devil said, "Come and worship me and I will give you the kingdoms of the world," Jesus responded, "It is written, you shall worship the Lord your God and Him only!" Jesus overcame by the Word. He was the Living Word and He used the Word to defeat Satan. Using the Word was entirely consistent with Jesus' nature. It was who He was. Jesus didn't quote some philosopher or Rabbi, He quoted Himself!

One of the most striking aspects of this story for me is the fact that Jesus remained absolutely consistent under pressure. After fasting and praying in the heat of the desert for forty days He must have been at His lowest ebb physically and emotionally. It was then when the devil struck and tried to outwit Him. Yet Jesus remained resolute in His commitment to God's truth. It begs the question: how consistent are we, especially when we come under pressure? The Bible says that a double-minded person is unstable in all his/her ways. If you behave one way at church and another way at home, then you are an unstable person. The apostle Peter wavered when he tried to keep both his Jewish and his Gentile friends happy, but Paul challenged him: "Be who you are!"

When we come under pressure, be it an attack on our health, our finances, or when we are tested morally, do we remain true to God's Word or do we waver? Do we quote the Word as Jesus did, or do people hear our emotions talking? "Why is this happening to me? It's not fair! I'm upset. I don't feel like going to church." This is not the way a mature Christian reacts to pressure. Life's hardships and trials only throw us off track when we are spiritually immature and we are spiritually immature if we don't eat God's Word. People who spend large amounts of time in the Bible grow up. In life there are some things we like and some things we don't; occasionally things seem to attack us. But we can overcome by the Word of God!

Jesus defended Himself purely by quoting the Word. So then the devil had a problem with the Word and not with Jesus! Always let the devil have a problem with the Word and not with you. Don't get into a debate with him and start arguing. He'll take it personally. When you stick rigidly to what the Word of God says then the devil's embarrassment and offence is with God. I love the devil getting offended with God. Every time he does it he is that bit nearer to hell.

It is the same with preaching. When you preach God's Word faithfully and people get offended, really they are offended with God. If I preach what David Carr thinks about how you should conduct your life, then you can be justifiably offended by it; if I preach what our church thinks about certain issues, you can be offended by that. But if I preach accurately what the Word of God says about your lifestyle then you can only be offended with God! It is the "sharp" tool of the Word piercing your heart as God begins to operate on your life.

Sound doctrine

Looking again the 2 Timothy scripture quoted earlier we read that the inspired Word of God provides us with "doctrine" for life. Doctrine may be defined as "a belief (or system of beliefs) accepted as authoritative" or "fundamental principles which guide you in fulfilling your objectives". Someone else has described doctrines as "guideposts that help you decide what to do in a given situation".

"All Scripture is given by inspiration of God, and is profitable for doctrine..."

(2 Timothy 3:16)

During the Charismatic renewal there have been those who have rejected a focus upon doctrine, thinking that all they needed was more of the Holy Spirit. I believe this has fostered a spiritual immaturity among many Charismatic believers. It shows how ignorant we can be at times, because it is the Holy Spirit who teaches us doctrine. Doctrine is the foundation of our faith. We need sound doctrine so that we can make sound judgements when we are faced with choices in life. The Bible doesn't give us a blow by blow account of how to deal with every specific situation we will find ourselves in – it gives us principles to put into practice. With the help of the Holy Spirit we have the wisdom to know how to apply the principles of doctrine in any circumstance.

Many Christians, if put on the spot and asked to summarise the doctrines of their faith, would be hard pressed to give a cogent response. Even the most well-established, mature Christian could be embarrassed in this situation. Yet, doctrine is what we build our lives upon and the Bible insists we should be able to give a reason for the hope that is within us. It is great to be able to say, "I know Jesus has changed me because I feel different," but that's not doctrine. Doctrine is the scriptural guide to who God is, what He is doing and what His objectives are. It sets the boundaries for our faith.

At this point I must commend the established Church

for its efforts to make doctrine known to the masses. Centuries ago when the majority of the people were not as well educated as they are today, the Church established the Apostle's Creed and the Nicene Creed to be verbal statements which would summarise the central doctrines of the Christian faith. They are worth repeating here as a simple, straightforward declaration of what Christians believe. The Apostle's Creed is so called because it is considered to be a true summary of the beliefs of the apostles themselves:

I believe in God, the Father almighty,
creator of heaven and earth.

I believe in Jesus Christ, God's only Son,
     our Lord,
who was conceived by the Holy Spirit,
born of the Virgin Mary,
suffered under Pontius Pilate,
was crucified, died, and was buried;
he descended to hell.
On the third day he rose from the dead;
he ascended into heaven,
he is seated at the right hand of the Father,
and he will come again to judge the living and
     the dead.

I believe in the Holy Spirit,
the holy catholic church,
the communion of saints,
the forgiveness of sins,
the resurrection of the body,
and the life everlasting. Amen.

Creeds were usually written to make a clear statement of truth in order to counter unbiblical ideas that were going around at the time. This is what most of Paul's New Testament letters set out to achieve. At the time that the Apostle's Creed was written, Gnosticism was having a damaging effect by spreading erroneous teaching among the early believers. The Creed was written to stamp out this heresy.

The Creed begins, "I believe in God, the Father almighty, creator of heaven and earth," since Gnostics insisted that the physical universe was evil and God did not create it. It continues by saying, "I believe in Jesus Christ, God's only Son, our Lord, who was conceived by the Holy Spirit, born of the Virgin Mary..." because the Gnostics claimed that Christians were wrong in thinking that God had taken a human form. There was a division of opinion even among the Gnostics themselves, but many believed that Jesus was never a man at all, that he only had the "appearance" of a man. The Creed points out that Jesus suffered under Pontius Pilate because at the time there were many myths being spread around about deities who had died and been resurrected. These stories were woolly and vague at best. No one ever seemed to be able to pinpoint exactly when and where their deity had died. The Creed is definite in its statement that Jesus died at a particular place and time in history under the jurisdiction of an identifiable ruler, Pontius Pilate, Governor of the Roman province of Judea from AD 26 until around AD 36, who was in power during the last ten years of the reign of Emperor Tiberius. Later the Creed mentions the need for the forgiveness of sins because the Gnostics argued that what man needed was not forgiveness, but enlightenment ... and so it goes on.

The Nicene Creed is still the most widely accepted creed in the Christian Church. It takes a very similar line to the Apostle's Creed, but expands some of the points:

> We believe in one God,
> the Father, the Almighty,
> maker of heaven and earth,
> of all that is, seen and unseen.

> We believe in one Lord, Jesus Christ,
> the only son of God,
> eternally begotten of the Father,
> God from God, Light from Light,
> true God from true God,
> begotten, not made,
> of one being with the Father.
> Through him all things were made.
> For us and for our salvation
> he came down from heaven:
> by the power of the Holy Spirit
> he became incarnate from the Virgin Mary,
> and was made man.
> For our sake he was crucified under Pontius
>   Pilate;
> he suffered death and was buried.
> On the third day he rose again
> in accordance with the Scriptures;
> he ascended into heaven
> and is seated at the right hand of the Father.

He will come again in glory
to judge the living and the dead,
and his kingdom will have no end.

We believe in the Holy Spirit, the Lord, the giver
of life,
who proceeds from the Father [and the Son].
With the Father and the Son
he is worshipped and glorified.
He has spoken through the Prophets.
We believe in one holy catholic and apostolic
Church.
We acknowledge one baptism for the forgiveness
of sins.
We look for the resurrection of the dead,
and the life of the world to come. Amen.

When the Apostle's Creed was written it was mostly countering Gnostic heresy, and when the Nicene Creed was written it was mostly countering Arianism which denied that Jesus was fully God. Arius was a Christian priest who taught that God the Father and God the Son were not co-eternal and that the Father had created the Son – a view completely at odds with the truth of the Trinity.

For me these Creeds illustrate the importance of the *logos* Word of God – the written Word – and how vital it is that we know what we believe and why. Without a firm understanding of what we believe, it is easy to get off track. In the next section of this book I will look at the *rhema* Word of God – the spoken or "now" Word that can help direct and guide us as we seek to walk with Him.

Word – Part 2

Every revival in the history of the Church has been characterised by an increased emphasis on the Word of God. In the previous section we looked at the *logos* or written Word of God. We saw how Jesus the Living Word came and walked among us clothed in humanity, causing the Old Testament to be fulfilled and creating the spark that generated the New Testament writings. We also explored the fact that the Word gives us our doctrine – the boundaries and central beliefs of our faith.

> **"When we come under the discipline of the Word and do things God's way, it affords us an unsurpassed freedom and security."**

As well as being a rich source of comfort and blessing in times of need, God's Word also has the ability to rebuke our behaviour and correct us when necessary as the Holy Spirit uses it to shape our character. No one likes being rebuked, but the Bible says it is necessary. Simply put, the Word shows us the difference between right and wrong. It shows us the correct way to conduct ourselves as children of God by doing three things:

- It reveals the fullness of God's will to us
- It disciples us
- It trains us in the way we should go

When we come under the discipline of the Word and do things God's way, it affords us an unsurpassed freedom and security. Rather than feeling afflicted by some heavy discipline, we are released. King David wrote,

> *"Your rod and Your staff, they comfort me."*
> (Psalm 23:4)

God makes a number of statements regarding discipline that do not sit comfortably with the politically correct philosophy of modern society. God asks the question, "Is there a father who would not discipline his children?" (Hebrews 12:7). Sadly, the answer is, yes, plenty of them! In this day and age a lack of fatherly discipline has spawned a rebellious generation. But this "hands off" approach is in stark contrast to the guidance of God's Word. God insists that if you don't discipline your children it is as good as saying they are not your own. You may have fathered your children genetically, but without loving discipline you are not being a father to them.

The Bible says that,

> *"For whom the LORD loves He corrects,*
> *Just as a father the son in whom he delights."*
> (Proverbs 3:12)

And Hebrews 12:6–13 in the New Living Translation gives us this incisive summary of God's desire to Father us and discipline us for fruitfulness:

> " 'For the Lord disciplines those he loves,
>   and he punishes those he accepts as his
>   children.'
>
> As you endure this divine discipline, remember that God is treating you as his own children. Whoever heard of a child who was never disciplined? If God doesn't discipline you as he does all of his children, it means that you are illegitimate and are not really his children after all. Since we respect our earthly fathers who disciplined us, should we not all the more cheerfully submit to the discipline of our heavenly Father and live forever?
>
> For our earthly fathers disciplined us for a few years, doing the best they knew how. But God's discipline is always right and good for us because it means we will share in his holiness. No discipline is enjoyable while it is happening – it is painful! But afterward there will be a quiet harvest of right living for those who are trained in this way.
>
> So take a new grip with your tired hands and stand firm on your shaky legs. Mark out a straight path for your feet. Then those who follow you, though they are weak and lame, will not stumble and fall but will become strong."

Many today, who live in a generation that submits itself to little or no discipline either individually or corporately, seek to justify their errant behaviour by labelling it with medical conditions. With respect to those who genuinely do have medical problems, I believe many have labelled their children with ADHD (Attention Deficit Hyperactivity Disorder) when really they are suffering for the lack of loving discipline. If a child is given to swearing at people and hitting out at his teachers it may be the cause of a psychological or physical illness – but it may be that the child has never received the love, attention and discipline he or she craves. It may be nothing to do with illness, but a simple lack of parental control.

Just as good parental discipline seems to be slipping away from society, in a similar way I see a lack of discipline in the Christian Church. Where are the shepherds who will lovingly correct and guide their flock? They are too busy running around trying to keep everyone happy! We suffer from ADHD syndrome in the Church too. I call it "Attention Demonic Hyper-Spiritual Disorder"!

- *Attention* – because unless people get it they leave
- *Demonic* – because they always blame a demon!
- *Hyper-Spiritual* – because they're always seeing visions
- *Disorder* – because they need their heads slapping!

Much of the Church has become just too consumer-driven. People go to church for what they can get out of it, not for what they can put into it, and a lack of godly discipline from church leaders has allowed them to get away with it. This, I believe, is where the Word of God is vital. If we preach faithfully the text of the Bible then it will impact people's lives; it will bring rebuke, discipline and correction; the Word will do its work and people's lives will be transformed. But we must be faithful to the Word.

When David wrote about the "Word" he said, *"He leads me in the paths of righteousness for His name's sake"* (Psalm 23:3). Righteousness is indicative of Christian living. Understanding something of the failure of his father David, Solomon declared in Proverbs that those who stray sexually, like his Dad did, from the paths of righteousness and live in covenant with unmarried people lose touch with the paths of righteousness unless they repent.

> *"Who forsakes the companion of her youth,*
> *And forgets the covenant of her God.*
> *For her house leads down to death,*
> *And her paths to the dead;*
> *None who go to her return,*
> *Nor do they regain the paths of life –*
> *So you may walk in the way of goodness,*
> *And keep to the paths of righteousness."*
>
> (Proverbs 2:17–20)

The Word of God is a lamp that will bring light to our path in life so that we will not fall into such errors as Solomon describes above. When we know "the Word" – both the written Scripture and Christ the Living Word – the Word walks us into the way of goodness.

I don't know any believer who can live a good Christian life without a sound knowledge of the Word.

Without the Bible's correction it is easy to stray from the right path. The Word keeps us in righteousness. There have been numerous examples of adultery among church leaders and yet the Bible says we should be content with the wife of our youth. God drummed that scripture into me years ago and it has saved me from going astray.

> *"... rejoice with the wife of your youth ...*
> *Let her breasts satisfy you at all times;*
> *And always be enraptured with her love."*
>
> (Proverbs 5:18–19)

The Bible is very explicit about these things. It doesn't mince its words; it is direct and to the point! It basically says, let your wife's breasts turn you on and don't go staring at anyone else's! Don't be diverted off the path of righteousness by another woman's plunging neckline. Please don't be offended by this – it's in the Word!

Logos and *rhema*

Throughout the New Testament there are two Greek words used to render the English "word" – *logos* and *rhema*. Until now all my discussions have revolved around the logos. Logos has an extraordinarily wide range of meanings. At its heart it means, "reason, discourse, speech", and even "meaning". Because of this, logos can refer to a word, a spoken phrase, or a thought that conveys something of meaning to the person who reads/hears it. It can take the form of a story, a narrative, a theory, a rule of conduct. All that is written in the Bible is logos. It is the inspired words of God written down that, when read and absorbed, are life changing because logos is literally "the speech of God".

The logos of the Bible represents what God is saying to us all generally. When the Bible commands us to love God with all our hearts, that applies to every one of us. A *rhema* word, on the other hand, is a word that God speaks *personally* to you. There are time in life when God speaks directly to us. Many people can testify to the fact that at times in their life when they were in despair, the rhema word of God came to them and had a lasting impact. Another person hearing that word would not have been impacted in the same way, but for the person who needed it, it was life changing. Rhema words happen when God takes a portion of Scripture and by the power of His Holy Spirit brings it to life for you now. The revelation that was *logos* to us all, now becomes *rhema* specifically for you.

Years ago after having a major heart scare, God spoke to me powerfully through a rhema word. On 2nd September 1987 I was taken into hospital after having a heart attack whilst driving on the motorway. Lying on the bed in the intensive care unit I looked for a Bible. It so happened that the Bible to hand was the Living Bible. As I lay there, wondering what would happen to me, on a drip with monitors stuck all over me, I felt the Lord say to me, "Look up Revelation 2:10." I read the verse. What I read was astounding to

me and no other version of the Bible puts it quite the
way the Living Bible does:

> *"Stop being afraid of what you are about to suffer
> for the devil will soon throw some of you into
> prison to test you. You will be persecuted for ten
> days. Remain faithful even when facing death and
> I will give you the crown of life and unending
> glorious future."*

Having read this, I asked the Ward Sister, "How long
am I going to be in here?"

"It's a mandatory ten days," she replied. I smiled.
Then I remembered that I was the top salesman for the
insurance company Crown Life! It was as if God was
saying to me, "Don't worry, you'll be in here for ten
days. After that you can return to your job at Crown
Life – they won't try to get rid of you." Was this a
coincidence or was it a rhema word from God? I
believe God was speaking directly to me.

I was called to the work of ministry in Solihull that
I still serve today because of a rhema word from God.
Every time a major decision needs to be made in our
church we look for a rhema word as well as a logos
word from God – and the two must never contradict
each other. Because God spoke to me clearly about
what I am to do, I am totally focused upon it and
refuse to be sidetracked. Sometimes people have
accused me of not having a world-view. This isn't
strictly true, and as a church we gladly give money
to missions, it is simply that God has called me to
establish His kingdom in Solihull. At the age of

nineteen the Lord spoke to me from Ezekiel chapter 33 and said, "I have made you a watchman over your own nation." Over the years I have been invited to pastor churches in Australia, New Zealand, South Africa and America, but I've turned every one down because I had a rhema word from God. I couldn't go because God had spoken. Forty-two years have elapsed since God spoke that word to me, but His word remains the same.

So, if God has the ability to speak words of guidance directly to us, why do we still need to read the Bible all the time? We read the Bible because it is the logos that enables us to live in the rhema. God doesn't hand out rhema words to us every day, they are fairly rare. We need to read the Bible to receive God's general guidance for living life and obeying Him.

Once I was invited to speak at a prophetic conference. There were five other speakers, all with prophetic ministries. Because of bringing all these ministries together and calling it a prophetic conference there was naturally an expectancy among the people that we would all prophesy the whole time and give words of direction and encouragement to people. Eventually I became frustrated with this attitude and got up at the next meeting and said, "Thus sayeth the Lord – read your Bible and sort yourself out!" At the very end of the conference I was chatting to another one of the speakers when a guy approached us. "Oh," he said, "I've got two prophets for the price of one! Could you give me a word?" Before my fellow speaker could respond I grabbed the Bible from under his arm and held it out to the man. "Here's the Word of the Lord," I said. "Read it and you just might get a word!" As far as prophetic ministry goes, men should only confirm what God is already saying to you. If you are depending on receiving a "word" from a prophet to give you guidance, then it is pretty likely you are not taking the time to listen to God for yourself.

When our church decided to become part of the Free Methodist denomination God gave us certain scripture verses that confirmed what He was saying to us. On top of that, three men of God from different parts of the world, none of whom knew about our discussions, came to me independently and gave me words just like the one God had already given me. These rhema words are great as confirmations of the fact you are hearing God correctly, but we must never be directed by them solely.

Faith comes by hearing the Word

When the written Word of God first came into being only the ten commandments existed. They came about essentially because the people of God wanted endorsement. Yet the commandments revealed the divine nature of the Almighty and His desire to bless His people. However, when God gave them the ten commandments as a kind of benchmark for their holiness, they found that they couldn't keep any of them! The Bible says that the letter kills, but the Spirit brings life. Man is fallen and by himself cannot uphold the law of God, but thank God that through Jesus, who came and fulfilled all the righteous requirements of the law, we can rely on the power of the Holy Spirit and are able to live a holy life.

> **"Your faith increases as you hear the Word preached and as you read your Bible ... Faith doesn't come by having a warm, tingling feeling when someone prays for you."**

Romans 10:17 explains that our faith will increase as we continue to read and absorb the Word of God. That's why it is so important to keep a regular Bible reading discipline:

> *"Faith comes by hearing, and hearing by the word of God."*

Your faith increases as you hear the Word preached and as you read your Bible. Doing these things "births" faith in you. Faith doesn't come by having a warm, tingling feeling when someone prays for you. No! Even when bad things happen – it's raining, your car has broken down and your tax bill has arrived – your faith can soar as you read and inwardly digest the truth of God's Word and meditate on His faithfulness.

Guarding the Word

The Word of God is life-producing, but we must learn to "hide it" in our heart and guard the seed that God is sowing into our life. Jesus told a parable about the word of the kingdom and how different people receive it or react to it. In other words, He said that the seed of God's Word will produce a harvest in us according to our heart's true desire. For instance, Matthew 13:19-21 says,

> *"When anyone hears the word of the kingdom, and does not understand it, then the wicked one comes and snatches away what was sown in his heart. This is he who received seed by the wayside. But he who received the seed on stony places, this is he who hears the word and immediately receives it with joy; yet he has no root in himself, but endures only for a while ... "*

Jesus is describing people who, despite hearing His Word, don't retain it and gain the benefit they should. There are also those who, *"when tribulation or persecution arises because of the word, immediately he stumbles"* (verse 21). Or in other words, when persecution comes he says, "Stuff it!" and goes down the pub! The fact is, when you are a Christian and stand up for what the Word of God teaches, you are going to get some flack.

Jesus also spoke about those who hear the Word but allow it to be stifled by, *"the cares of this world ... "* (verse 22). So many things seem to crowd in and demand our time and attention these days it is easy to forget to prioritise God's Word. "I'm too busy running the kids around ... I've had a rough time lately ... I'm busy studying for my exams ... " all seem like valid excuses on the surface, but these "cares of this world" can rob us of time with God that would actually leave us better prepared to cope with them! Continuing in verse 22, Jesus couples this idea with that of, *"the deceitfulness of riches"*, which He says, *"choke the word"* and makes us *"unfruitful"*. How many have been sucked into the trap of pursuing a career, working all the hours imaginable, to get a better job to earn more money – and all to buy more stuff we don't need and to have better holidays that we don't enjoy because we are so stressed out! This is the deceit of riches – that material things can make you happy. If that was really true then the highest paid members of society would be the happiest – pop stars, footballers, city financiers etc. – and self-evidently these people are not! People say to me, "God wants me to be a success." My question is, for who? Make sure your motives are right. Watch out that you don't choke the Word. Don't rely on your own cleverness or you will become unfruitful.

If we do all that we can to make our lives fertile ground for receiving God's Word, then, Jesus says, we will receive immeasurable blessing:

> *"But he who received seed on the good ground is he who hears the word and understands it, who indeed bears fruit and produces: some a hundredfold, some sixty, some thirty."*
>
> (Matthew 13:23)

The key, Jesus says, is *understanding.* It is no good me standing up and preaching what I believe to be a great sermon unless you can understand it! The Word of God on its own does not change us and simply hearing *about* the truth does not change us – it is the *knowing* of the truth that sets us free – when the Word of God is not simply in our heads, but our hearts.

As powerful as the Word of God is, we can neutralise its effectiveness. Mark 7:13 says,

> "... *making the word of God of no effect through your tradition which you have handed down. And many such things you do.*"

I'm the first to admit that we don't always get it right as a church. Occasionally we make a *faux pas*. The fact is that when you are making cakes you sometimes get a flat one! The only way not to have a flat cake is to not bake cakes! But we do try not to make the Word of God ineffective by stifling it with traditions that don't mean anything. Some people get upset if church becomes too modern and contemporary, whilst others get upset if things remain too traditional. Both are entitled to their point of view, but traditions, if they become empty rituals, will kill us. We might turn up to church with spiked hair and body piercing and have our worship led by someone in ripped jeans, or we may turn up in our best suits and dresses and be greeted by a minister in formal robes – either will become dangerous to us when we are more interested in the format than the content!

We must never try to make a doctrine out of our church traditions. I once had a phone call from a man who said he needed to leave our church denomination

because we don't preach from the King James Bible.
"You're off beam," I told him. "Jesus didn't use the
King James version either. Sorry to prick your
balloon!" We can all have our preferences, but we
must not make them into things that destroy our
peace.

Jesus promised everlasting life to those who believed
in His Word:

> *"Most assuredly, I say to you, he who hears My
> word and believes in Him who sent Me has
> everlasting life, and shall not come into judgment,
> but has passed from death into life."*
>
> (John 5:24)

God's Word is so liberating. If you believe in what God
is saying then you don't need to feel condemned all the
time. But we must be wary of thinking that just by
reading the Bible regularly we are saved. As Jesus'
parable points out – it is possible to receive the Word
and let it be choked out by other concerns leaving us
fruitless. The Bible even speaks about those who
"search" the Scriptures, suggesting a much more
diligent reading of them, and hope to find eternal life
by filling their heads with knowledge about the Word.
No, eternal life belongs to those who *embrace* its
teaching.

> *"But you do not have His word abiding in you,
> because whom He sent, Him you do not believe.
> You search the Scriptures, for in them you think
> you have eternal life; and these are they which*

*testify of Me. But you are not willing to come to
Me that you may have life."*

(John 5:38–40)

This is a scary scripture. It means a person could,
technically, be reading their Bible and their daily
reading notes and not be born again. Even cults search
the Scriptures but do not know eternal life. The Word
has to be allowed to penetrate your heart; it needs to be
in you, on your lips, in your heart, in your mind. Then
the Word of God can transform you. Therefore, as we
move on as a church, we will not only be passionate
worshippers, but also willing containers of the Word.

The wonder of the Word

1 Peter 4:11 says that,

*"If anyone speaks, let him speak as the oracles of
God."*

The word "oracle" here means "utterance of God".
In other words, if anybody speaks, let him/her speak
God's words and not their own. Personally, I am far
more interested in what God has to say than other
people. People are too willing to offer their opinions
and they are often not helpful. If my wife had listened
to the advice of other Christians when she was younger
then she would not now be my wife! Human advice
can sometimes be helpful, and I am not suggesting that

we should not be accountable to one another, but what we really need to hear is God's advice. Consider this when you are tempted to give advice to someone: if God has not given you a word for that person then it's best to say nothing. People are too eager to speak prophetically into the lives of others and when that word originates from human wisdom, not the prompting of the Holy Spirit, all it does is to bring confusion. We need to know what God is truly saying to us and our first port of call should be His Word.

The Word of God is the truth. It is God's thoughts, intents and actions gathered together to inspire and transform us. No other authority than the Word is given to Church. This is the wonder of the Word. All of the following is true of the Word of God:

- We preach it and we believe it ... we read it, we live it, we love it, we teach it, we model it, we disciple people into it, we equip the saints for the work of the ministry in it, we prophesy according to it, we heal the sick in line with its commands. It won't pass away; it's eternal!
- It challenges, changes, convicts, convinces, converts, confirms, consoles, conditions, corrects, celebrates, conquers our life and its needs.
- It exalts, it equips, it evangelises the sheep of its pasture.
- It's full of revelation, revolution, redemption and righteousness.
- It brings us to healing, wholeness and hope.
- It sets us free from doubt, debt, disease, dishonour, debauchery, deception and divination.

- It leads us to delight, direction, discipleship, destiny!
- It becomes the love of our life, the language of our mouth, the lamp to our feet, the light to our way, the letter from our Father, the legacy to His children, the law of Heaven keeping me from the lust of Hell!
- It's the last word of authority!
- It's called the Word!

Revivals grow great preachers and teachers. The Word of God again becomes the focal point for pulpit and for pew! We preach not "share". Remember faith comes from hearing the Word and people can't hear unless a preacher be sent!

Wonders

It has been said that a miracle is the occurrence of any event apparently contradictory to, and unexplainable by, the laws of science. Miracles, or wonders, therefore, are usually attributed to God. They are events that seem to transcend the natural order of things and our human understanding of them.

If one thing is certain though, it is the fact that every believer, to one degree or another, wants to see the miraculous in the life of the Church. Yet, despite our longing for it, the miraculous is not widespread in our nation. Yes, there are pockets of amazing things happening, but we are a long way away from the outpouring of healings and miracles that has been so evident in historic revivals. Why is this? In this chapter I will try to offer some suggestions as to why this might be the case and also, I hope, raise our expectations of seeing more of the miraculous power of God at work in our nation.

In Isaiah chapter 7 we read a brief part of the story of Ahaz, king of Judah, who led God's people for a time. The story tells of a time when two rival kings are plotting to go up to Jerusalem and make war against it. Isaiah, the prophet, comes to Ahaz with a word from the Lord about how the plot will fail and says to Ahaz that God is saying to him, "Ask Me for a sign." Ahaz, however, is not a man of faith and does not know how to react. He is afraid and refuses to interact with Almighty God.

This is an interesting situation. Judah belongs to God, they are His people. Eventually Jesus would be born from the line of Judah. At this time, however, the man in charge of that line has no faith. He is not a God-fearing man and is occupying this position of power simply because of his family line. He came from good stock; his father was well known, as was his grandfather; they were men who knew the Lord; but Ahaz is just coasting along. He has no personal relationship with God, no belief in Him – yet, he is at the head of a godly nation.

I'm sad to say that I have come across a number of ministers who are in the same position as Ahaz, whether they realise it or not. They find themselves at the head of a group of godly people who, deep down, want to do God's will and go God's way, but like Ahaz the leaders are scared of what God might do if they give up the control of their church. They are frightened of what might happen if God breaks out. As a result, they lose their focus and their effectiveness.

Recently I had the opportunity to spend several hours in the company of a very well known actor and TV personality who is not a Christian. He commented to me that he had always thought of himself as an agnostic, rather than an atheist, but when he had read *The Power of Positive Thinking* by Norman Vincent Peale, it set him thinking that there might be more to

life and he decided to visit a church to see if there was
"anything to this 'God thing'". He said to himself,
"If the church has anything in it then I'll give up my
career and all my money and become a priest." Sadly,
he turned to me and said, "David, the church had
nothing to offer me."

This man's experience confirms what I already knew
to be true: you can appear to be in God's purposes, in
God's place, and yet have nothing to offer anyone –
just like Ahaz, who was the king of God's house, but
had no power, no faith and no belief. People say,
"I don't want to go to church, it's full of hypocrites."
Yes, it is! "I don't want to belong to a church because
churches fight amongst themselves." Yes, they do!
And, "The church looks like it's falling apart anyway."
You're right, it does!

But why then does the Church still exist after two
thousands years, even though man has let it down,
polluted it and abused it? Because the Church still
belongs to God and God will keep it! God blessed the
kingdom of Judah *despite* its shameful king. Similarly,
God loves and blesses His Church regardless of who is
running it. The Church is blessed because Jesus is the
Head! The reason why God still blesses the
institutionalised Church when there is so much
infighting is not because any one faction is right, but
because God is committed to building His Church. So,
if you have a successful church and think it's because
of you, think again. It's all about Jesus!

Ahaz was an unbelieving, ungodly man. He ruled
God's people and yet his trust in a miracle working
God was zero. Yet, at that moment, the nation needed a

miracle as two powerful kings conspired to attack and defeat Judah. Despite Ahaz's unbelief, God stepped in and acted on behalf of His people. Shortly after this incident, before the kings could wage war on Judah, they were both killed. One king, Rezin, was assassinated, and the other king, Pekah, was killed in battle – both in the same year.

> **"If God says there is a miracle over your life then there is a miracle waiting to happen."**

Inevitably, there will come times in our lives when it seems that there are people, situations, or circumstances, that are conspiring against us and trying to destroy us – just like the kings who conspired against Ahaz. It could be cancer, or bankruptcy, or problems in the family. You may be praying for a miracle and nothing seems to be happening. But don't be discouraged. It took two years before the Lord disposed of the enemies of Judah. If the Lord is on your side, then the answer to your prayers will surely come. The problem we suffer from in this day and age is that we want everything to happen instantly – instant food, instant sex, instant whatever we want. However, if God says there is a miracle over your life then there is a miracle waiting to happen. Some time ago we prayed for a lady at our church who had terminal cancer. God miraculously healed her, but the healing took place over a period of six months. The miracle was that she should have been dead long before her healing was complete.

People often say, "If only I saw miracles in the church again, I would come." But the fact is, we see miracles in our church on a weekly basis at our healing meetings, and although our church is growing rapidly, it's not full yet!

What I find very strange is that most Christians' expectation of the miraculous is very low indeed. I would go as far as to say there are some Christians who don't want miracles in their churches at all. The supernatural, for them, is not part of their spiritual experience, nor do they want it to be. But if God is the God of the miraculous – a Being whose very nature it is to keep on doing miraculous things – who are we to argue? Should we not have very high expectations of seeing miracles as part of our "ordinary" Christian experience?

Miracles are not common in the West at all, and part of the problem, I believe, is that so many people suffer from Ahaz's disease. Even with the great prophet Isaiah at his side, urging him to listen to what God was saying, the king still chose not to believe God. But, when we are confronted with a miracle working God we have a choice to make – we have to either embrace Him for Who He is, or reject Him, like Ahaz did.

There were four things that Isaiah told Ahaz he must do, and these four are relevant for us today if we are to see signs and wonders more frequently in the Western Church. All four phrases are taken from Isaiah 7:4.

1. "Take heed"

I believe God is saying to His people today, "Excuse Me, are you listening to Me?" Just as the Lord spoke to

the seven churches in the book of Revelation we need to "hear what the Spirit is saying to the Church".
I believe God wants to pour out His Spirit upon us in power, if only we will listen to Him and cooperate with His agenda. Any pastor will tell you that you preach your heart out to your congregation week after week and then a preacher comes over from the States and delivers one message and suddenly everyone says, "I've never heard this before – it's amazing!" You don't know whether to cry or shoot yourself because it's the same message you've been preaching for the last six weeks and the people haven't heard you!

There comes a time when God speaks to us and if we are not listening we miss out on what we could have had. God speaks to Ahaz through Isaiah and says, in effect, "Watch my lips. Take heed. Listen to what I am saying because I want to do a miracle for you." God is visiting us too and He wants to do miracles among us, but if we don't listen attentively to His voice and do what He tells us, we could miss being a part of it.

2. "Be quiet"

The Bible puts it politely, but often I imagine God saying to us, "Just shut up, will you!" We have so much to say for ourselves, but how much of what we say is really what is on God's heart? I believe God is saying to us today, "Be still and know that I am God. Stop striving and let Me move among you." Sometimes we are so busy speaking, so busy rushing around, that we miss the miracles God wants to do. We don't know how to simply be still, be quiet, and receive from Him. If you want to know what God wants to do for you, then be still, be quiet, and listen to what He is saying.

3. "Do not fear"

This is a big issue for many people and one which has quenched the Holy Spirit to a degree: fear – particularly the fear of not being in control; the fear of letting go and letting God be God. Some while ago I was ministering in the north of England in a town where there is a high concentration of Asian families. Many Asians turned up to our evening meetings and it was fascinating to see how they reacted to the moving of the Holy Spirit, compared to Westerners. One thing that took me by surprise was that they bowed to me because they considered me to be a "holy man" (it's not something that I'm insisting my home church start doing!). But, in prayer they stood calmly and were open and expectant. Even though all around them people were going down under the power of God, they were not afraid.

What a contrast that is to most Westerners. So often we debate and question, "Is this really of God? I'm not sure about it. Do I have to fall over?" What puzzles me is, why would God want to hurt you? Do you think He would do anything to you that would harm you in any way? Why not simply come to Him with open arms and see what He wants to do to bless you? That is how our Asian brothers and sisters approached Him. Why be frightened of receiving from God?

4. "Do not be fainthearted"

We give up too soon! I think many people miss out on the miraculous because they give up praying for it when they should push through to receive what they need. In our "instant" world, longevity and persistence seem to be a thing of the past. The Bible says that you will reap your reward in time if you don't give up. The whole point of Christianity is consistency and persistency. Often you have to hang in their for your miracle.

Some people say, "I was prayed for once but I didn't get healed." I think what prevents them from going for more prayer is the fear of disappointment. They don't want to be prayed for time and again with no results. But in the Bible we see gradual healings as well as instantaneous ones. Naaman had to dip himself in the river seven times before he was healed. One man who came to Jesus for healing was told to go and he would be healed on his way. Another man, Jesus had to pray for twice before he was fully healed. We should persist and hang in there if we want to see God move on our behalf.

The challenge to all of us is issued in Isaiah 7:9:

> "If you will not believe,
> Surely you shall not be established."

The word "established" here means to have a firm foundation that will stand the test of time. It is a solid foundation that leaves adequate room for expansion. It has similar connotations to a business putting a sign over its door or on its letterhead: "Established 1830". It tells you that the company has been long established, that they have a track record, and are around for the long haul. What God is saying to us through this verse, I believe, is that if we don't believe Him for signs and wonders, then we won't have a track record – we won't see much, if anything, of the miraculous taking place around us.

Notice that the command of this verse is "believe". Belief is different from faith. Isaiah didn't command King Ahaz to "have faith" because faith is a gift from God. Believing, however, is something that you and I have the capacity to do. Belief is the feeling of certainty we have when we know that something exists or is true. It is a mental act – you believe with your mind. Belief results from a mental acceptance of the conviction of the truth.

> **"As we continue to believe in God and trust in His ability to do what He says, we will see bigger and better miracles beginning to happen around us."**

King Ahaz was given the opportunity to receive a miracle. It is one of the few places in the Bible where God issues a challenge and invites a man to test the truth of what He is saying:

> *"Moreover the LORD spoke again to Ahaz, saying,*
> *'Ask a sign for yourself from the LORD your God.'"*
> (Isaiah 7:10–11)

There does come a time when God allows us to test Him. By "testing Him" we simply prove Him right. It isn't a stress test where one might jump up and down on something until it breaks! Testing God will always prove Him right, not wrong. In the same way, if God has given you a word about something and you know for sure that it is from Him, then you need to hold on to Him and not let go. Test Him and He will be proven right in the long run.

As we continue to believe in God and trust in His ability to do what He says, we will see bigger and better miracles beginning to happen around us. Unless you first believe God for a small miracle and begin to establish a track record, then you will never believe God to see a really big miracle. A person who has never had a miracle at all will struggle even to understand how they can relate to the miraculous.

God invited Ahaz to be part of the miracle He was about to accomplish, but Ahaz was scared and refused. What God does then is to bypass Ahaz and do the miracle regardless, but Ahaz is not to be a part of it. God is never deflated by our unbelief. He is committed to enacting His word, and if He has decreed a miracle is going to happen in the land, then it will happen.

I believe the same is true of our churches. There are some great churches in our nation, but many are not welcoming the miraculous working of God's power. They don't want that type of Christianity. If you just want a nice church that gives communion, reminds you that you are forgiven, and then delivers a nice word from the Bible – nothing too committed – then you are going to miss God! If you don't want a miracle from God then there will be a miracle without you. God will have to bypass you and continue about His purposes, but you will miss out.

Personally, I am not prepared to go there because I am a praying, miracle-believing person. I have often seen churches in our nation refuse to ask God for a sign because of unbelief and I don't want to be a part of that. The Christian faith is one of signs and wonders – we have a miracle working God on our side! Signs and wonders are for today and are not something that happened only in the early Church. Despite the view that many reformed theologians espouse, there is nothing in Scripture to give authority to the idea that miracles passed away after the formation of the Church. That will not happen until Jesus comes again for His Bride, the Church. Then, and only then, death and sickness, poverty, signs, wonders, speaking in tongues, and prophecy, will all pass away – but not before!

All throughout the Bible the wonders of God are spoken of. The Word of God is brimming over with examples of signs and wonders, because that's who God is! It is His very nature. In Exodus 3:20 He says,

> "I will stretch out My hand and strike Egypt with all My wonders which I will do in its midst; and after that he [Pharaoh] will let you go."

The Lord used signs and wonders to break the bondage of slavery in Egypt and release His people. He can do the same for us today, releasing incredible miracles that cause the enemy to retreat and release people from darkness and bondage. Later in Exodus we read this statement regarding the nature of God:

> *"Who is like You, O LORD, among the gods?*
> *Who is like You, glorious in holiness,*
> *Fearful in praises, doing wonders?"*
>
> (Exodus 15:11)

It was through signs and wonders that the children of Israel came out of Egypt; it was through signs and wonders they went through the wilderness; it was through signs and wonders that they were led to the Promised Land.

> *"And Joshua said to the people, 'Sanctify yourselves, for tomorrow the LORD will do wonders among you.'"*
>
> (Joshua 3:5)

Just as Joshua called for the people of God to sanctify themselves, we, the Church, need to sanctify ourselves and be ready to receive a mighty intervention of the Holy Ghost!

Recently in America a survey was conducted in which 84% of the people interviewed said that they believed God performed miracles, and 48% claimed to have had one. We need to raise our expectations for God to do wonders in our midst. God has acted on behalf of every believer throughout history. For Joshua He stopped the sun! He enabled Peter to walk on water. He parted the Red Sea for Moses. The dead were raised. Three young men miraculously survived the blistering heat of a furnace. A widow's oil never ran out.

Daniel wrote,

> *"How great **are** His signs,*
> *And how mighty His wonders!*
> *His kingdom **is** an everlasting kingdom,*
> *And His dominion **is** from generation to*
> *   generation."*
>
> (Daniel 4:3, emphasis added)

And through the prophet Joel the Lord said,

> *"And I will show wonders in the heavens and in*
> *   the earth:*
> *Blood and fire and pillars of smoke."*
>
> (Joel 2:30)

Finally, Jesus said,

> *"Most assuredly, I say to you, he who believes in*
> *Me, the works that I do he will do also; and **greater***
> ***works** than these he will do, because I go to My*
> *Father."*
>
> (John 14:12, emphasis added)

Miracles are given to us as an aid, to help us believe. Miracles are also evident wherever the kingdom of God is manifest, pushing back the boundaries of darkness:

> *"Then fear came upon every soul, and many*
> *wonders and signs were done through the*
> *apostles."*
>
> (Acts 2:43)

What type of church do we want to belong to? Surely, it must be one that believes in the Word of God and believes that the results of preaching it are signs and wonders. The Word of God is active and living, it has power today, and we should believe that miracles will follow as we are faithful in speaking it out. I believe in a wonder-working Church and that we will see more and more of the miraculous in the days ahead. During the Wesley revival the preaching of the Word was followed by many miracles, signs, wonders and healings.

Wealth

Now we come to the fourth attribute of a church in revival – wealth – something that many people in the Church fail to understand and many people in the world abuse. There is no revival that does not bring, first of all, a wealth towards God, a wealth with God, and a wealth from God to His people, but the fact is, revivals need to be bought and paid for. A revival may break out because of a divine spark, because God initiates a move of His Spirit, but to continue a move of God finance is needed. "Money" need not be a dirty word as far as the Church is concerned.

> **"Revivals need to be bought and paid for."**

To have "wealth" means to possess riches or be in a position of ease. Contrary to the two extreme perspectives of Christian teaching on wealth, the Bible never teaches that believers should hold on to either universal poverty or universal prosperity. Neither extreme should be our goal. It is not a case of which is better – a Rolex or a bread roll – the two are not in competition. The secret all believers need to learn is the lesson of the apostle Paul, who said, "I have learnt to be content with little or much." That is the balance we all need to have. Prosperity, and sometimes wealth, should be an integral part of our Christlikeness. It is never a formula to be worked out, but a lifestyle that comes from God.

Solomon was reputed to be one of the richest men in the world, as well as one of its wisest. God gave him the gift of wisdom and he used it in many difficult situations. I have always found that the best advice comes from people who have been there before us and know where it's at. Who better then to listen to on the subject of finance than one of the richest men in the world, Solomon?

The thing we must always remember about Solomon is that he became rich because he chose wisdom. Possessing vast wealth does not make you a wise person. When God offered Solomon anything he wanted, he asked for great wisdom. God gave it to him and also blessed him with incredible wealth to go along with it. So, what insights does Solomon have to offer us when it comes to wealth?

In Ecclesiastes 5:9 he says,

> *"Moreover the profit of the land is for all; even the king is served from the field."*

I have had the privilege of travelling a great deal and consequently I have eaten all over the world. Some of the more salubrious venues have included the Hotel de Paris in Monte Carlo and on the Orient Express. It was great food, but the fact is, the potatoes came from the same ground as they did for the person who has fish and chips from the chip shop round the corner. The soil is no different; it's the same ground. The difference in price is all down to the environment the food is prepared in and who is preparing it. No one pays for the food – who would pay £40 for a potato? You pay for the man who cooked it. The point is, sometimes in life we will have the opportunity to dine like a king; more often than not, it could be the chip shop instead. Whatever it is, we need to live with an attitude of thankfulness for God's provision.

Solomon also said,

> "He who loves silver will not be satisfied with
>   silver;
> Nor he who loves abundance, with increase.
> This also is vanity.
> When goods increase,
> They increase who eat them."
>
> (Ecclesiastes 5:10–11)

Remember, Solomon had immeasurable wealth, so he knew what he was talking about. He says that if we run after accumulating more and more stuff, it will never satisfy us. We will just want more and more. We can see this is true. Isn't it so that when we receive a pay rise, within six months we have gradually increased our standard of living until we are living up to the level of our income? Isn't it true that when we are living in a three-bedroom house we tell ourselves that life would be so much better if only we had a four-bedroom house? But not long after we get our four-bedroom house we are running out of room again because we have expanded to fill the available space. In fact our problems are mitigated because we've bought more and more "stuff" to fill our house with!

Solomon continues this thought to say,

> *"When goods increase,*
> *They increase who eat them;*
> *So what profit have the owners*
> *Except to see them with their eyes?*
>
> *The sleep of a labouring man is sweet."*
>
> (Ecclesiastes 5:11–12)

What does he mean? A man who does an honest day's work will have nothing to worry about. But, he warns,

> *"The abundance of the rich will not permit him*
> *to sleep."*
>
> (Ecclesiastes 5:12)

If you have placed your trust in God and seek to offer Him an honest day's work, that is an incredibly liberating place to be. If, actually, you are trusting in your personal wealth, or your own abilities, then you will go to bed at night worried in case you lose it all on the stock market next week, or that a business competitor is going to undercut you on a deal, etc. I had first-hand experience of this when I worked in football management and before that in the insurance business. I dealt with some very wealthy people and the majority of them were paranoid about their money.

Our wealth belongs to God

Another telling insight from Solomon is this:

> *"There is a severe evil which I have seen under the*
> *sun:*
> *Riches kept for their owner to his hurt.*
> *But those riches perish through misfortune."*
>
> (Ecclesiastes 5:13–14)

Here is revealed one of the great biblical secrets of a truly abundant life: material wealth is not for us to hold on to, but to release for the blessing of others, and especially to resource God's kingdom. Wealth doesn't belong really belong to us in the first place – it belongs to God. When we hold on to the riches that God places in our hands, we stifle them and they begin to diminish; they don't bear fruit as they should.

There is also a salutary reminder of our mortality that puts the issue of wealth into perspective:

> *"When he begets a son, there is nothing in his hand.*
> *As he came from his mother's womb, naked shall*
> *he return,*
> *To go as he came;*
> *Ad he shall take nothing from his labour*
> *Which he may carry away in his hand."*
>
> (Ecclesiastes 5:14–15)

It's an old story, but highly appropriate: two grave diggers are leaning on their spades as an impressive funeral cortège passes by, the hearse flanked by Rolls Royces (I have actually attended a funeral that had fourteen family owned Rolls'!). One grave digger comments to his mate, "Wow, he was rich. I wonder how much he left?" "Everything!" his colleague replied.

This is very true, but I want to take a diversion for a moment and pick up on another nugget of godly wisdom in those verses from our "financial advisor" Solomon: *"When he begets a son, there is nothing in his hand."* It seems to me that many a son with a wealthy father has gone off the rails because his father failed to teach him the true meaning of wealth. It is a mistake I hope we, the Church, don't make with the emerging generation. If you don't make your son work for a living and hand him wealth on a plate, it is very likely he will lose everything you gave him. Why? Because it was never his in the first place.

I have seen a number of wealthy people hand businesses over to their sons, but if the son is not really capable of running it, then it will begin to fail as wrong decisions are made. I made the decision long ago that if I carried on in business and my son wanted to follow in my footsteps, I would send him to work for a competitor first to learn the business the hard way, making mistakes and taking the knocks, just like I did. Then, if he proved he could do it, he would earn the right to run my business. But he wouldn't just "inherit" my business because he'd got my name. That is a very dangerous thing.

I once had a conversation with a very well-known entertainer who told me that he had bought each of his children a flat and a car. "That's all they will ever get from me," he said, "and they are on their own now. If I didn't do that, then they would be layabouts for the rest of their lives." He added, "When I die there will be enough for them, but I hope to live a long time, so they'll have to be poverty stricken until then unless they fend for themselves." I thought to myself, "What a man of integrity." He is training his children to know the real value of wealth.

Being satisfied with what we have

Unless your "wealth" comes out of your relationship with Christ, then you will never have enough. What is "enough" anyway? Who can define it? But when Christ is our central focus, all our needs are met and we are satisfied. We have more than enough. Going back to my football days, I saw over and over again that people were never satisfied with what they had.

Footballers are amongst the most insecure professionals in any sphere of life because of the fickle nature of the sport. The average footballer's career lasts just eight years. Many players retire at thirty-five, but it is very difficult to stay at the top of the game even for that long. Hence, they are always worrying about their income and what they are going to live off when they are forced to retire. I negotiated with some very well known football managers to arrange contracts for numbers of young players. I remember one time I got a young lad a very good package and he was really grateful, thanking me over and over, "Dave, you're fantastic. I couldn't have wished for anything better. Thank you."

Soon after I had done that deal, I negotiated a package for another young player with the same club and managed to get him a slightly better deal because he was a forward (forwards tend to earn more because they are the chief goal scorers). Before I knew it, the first player (a defender) was on the phone to me. Footballers are unique in the fact that they all discuss and know one another's salaries. I can't imagine it happening in any other sphere of business! This young man complained bitterly to me that he was unhappy and wanted a transfer to another club. "Why?" I asked, "You've only just joined!" "Because," he said, "so and so is getting paid more than me!" I was very firm with him and said, "Listen fellah, a couple of weeks ago you were very happy with what you'd got. You are only discontent because of what this other guy has got!"

Jesus identified this "wealth jealously" syndrome when He told a parable about some workers who had been hired to bring in the harvest. The boss agreed a fee for the job with the first workers he hired: "I'll give you £50 for the day." They were happy with that and began to work. The boss could soon see, however, that more labour was needed and so at 3.00pm he went out into the marketplace to round up some more workers. "I tell you what," he said to them, "I'll give you £50 each if you'll work until 6.00pm."

"OK, it's a deal," they said.

At the end of the day, when it came time to pay the workers, the boss called in those who had done just a few hours' work and paid them their £50. Noticing this, the people who had been working all day thought to themselves that they must have a bonus coming. "After all," they reasoned, "we've been labouring all day. Those other fellows have only worked three hours." However, the boss only gave each of them the agreed £50.

"Hang on," protested the workers. "How come those guys got paid the same as us and we've been working all day?" The boss would have none of it. "Friends, we agreed a price at the beginning and that is what you have been paid. You were happy with it at the beginning. You are only discontent now because your heart is wrong" (paraphrased from Matthew 20:1–16).

As an employee, do you think you are being paid what you are worth? "What does it matter if someone gets paid more than you?" Jesus says, "It's all my money!" There is a principle here. If you sign the contract and agree to the wages, then stop beefing about someone who has better negotiation skills and gets paid more than you do! If you are as good as you think you are, then your company won't want to lose you. Good people will always eventually get paid what they are worth. Companies can't afford to lose great employees.

Wealth is a heritage from God

Solomon says in verse 19,

> *"As for every man to whom God has given riches and wealth, and given him power to eat of it, to*

receive his heritage and rejoice in his labour – this is the gift of God."

(Ecclesiastes 5:19)

He makes another telling point: God does not give riches to every person. Some get more than others. Certain individuals are blessed with immense wealth while others are not. This verse must surely cause trouble for individuals on both sides of the theological wealth debate. Those who believe that all Christians should reject wealth and be poor are in trouble here, because clearly, there are those to whom God gives riches. They don't necessarily make it for themselves because they are clever business people, God gives it to them. Conversely, those who belong to the "name it and claim it" camp are also in trouble. God blesses some with riches, and therefore, necessarily, there are those whom He does not! The Lord gives, but He also takes away. There is no universalism in God's kingdom when it comes to material gain, except for the fact that He promises to supply all our needs.

> **"It is the destiny of all Christians to be 'wealthy', but we misunderstand true wealth."**

When God blesses us He gives us more than wealth, He gives us a heritage. In other words, He doesn't give us something temporary – money is quickly used and needs to be replenished frequently! A heritage is something that lasts. Some people make money and they lose it overnight, but when God makes you wealthy He also adds the ability to keep that wealth. The person who lives purely for wealth will be controlled by it; it will dominate his/her thinking. But the person who lives for God and has kingdom interests as their priority will have wealth as a reward as they live in the blessing of God.

It is the destiny of all Christians to be "wealthy", but we misunderstand true wealth. It doesn't mean we will all be rolling in money, but we will be blessed, cared for by God and have more than enough. Wealth stems from our relationship with Christ. Like God, we can be rich in mercy, rich in faith. The people who know that these are true riches are the ones God is most likely to trust with material wealth!

Unless you have wealth within, then external wealth will always overtake you and dominate you. First, we must be rich towards God. I believe that some people, if they were to receive great wealth, would be backslidden and nowhere in their faith within six months, because they have failed to develop a "richness" of relationship with God. Wealth would corrupt them because they are poor inside.

Years ago I made a decision – and I don't make this claim out of a sense of pride or boastfulness – that I would be satisfied and thankful for whatever God blessed me with and I chose not to go the route of accumulating more and more material things – even though I had a very highly paid job and could have easily afforded to do it. If you ever want to buy me a present, you will have difficulty, because I never want anything. Ask my wife, she will tell you it's true! Every year she asks me what I want for my birthday and I say, "I don't know. Nothing really!" Am I so well off that I have everything I could ever need? No. It's simply that I have taken a decision to be satisfied with what I have.

Being in the football business I drove a succession of big, expensive cars. When I left to be a full-time pastor I needed to find a new car, so I went to buy a nice small one. Someone from the church saw me getting out of it and commented to me, "You can't drive that car Pastor, it's not your image." I said, "Well, you don't know my image in that case. I'll drive whatever I'm given. It doesn't bother me!" Today I am blessed because a kind person was directed by the Lord to give me an amazing deal on a BMW. But I never went around confessing that the Lord was going to bless me with a great car, a great house etc. I don't need such trappings to convey to people how the Lord has prospered me. In fact, I was so embarrassed to be driving a BMW at first, that it took me some time to overcome it and not feel uncomfortable. In the end we have to receive whatever blessing God decides to pour out on us.

The point I am making is, you cannot "buy" a man who is not motivated by money. Years ago, at the height of my business activities, Molly and I took a conscious decision to walk away from the opportunity to buy and live in a one million pound home. Why? Because I realised that I was going to be a pastor to some poor people as well as some well-off people, and I could not expect a poor person to come to my lavish home where I would say to them, "I know what you are going through." It wouldn't have been wrong for me to have a house like that and I make no judgement about those who do. God has blessed them and rewarded them. But I made a decision based on a revelation from the Holy Spirit that it would not help me as a pastor.

Every Christian has a promise from God that He will look after us and provide for us as we trust in Him. Psalm 37:25 says,

> *"I have been young, and now am old;*
> *Yet I have not seen the righteous forsaken,*
> *Nor his descendants begging bread."*

God will never let His own go begging. We can stay in His promises and live in His provision. God's children are not destined to be like the poor people that Solomon mentions:

> *"God has given to some men very great wealth and*
> *honour so that they can have everything they want,*
> *yet he doesn't give them the health to enjoy it and*
> *they die, and others get it all."*
>
> (Ecclesiastes 6:2, TLB)

How awful! How absurd! What a hollow mockery that is. Wealth devoid of God's blessing is like owning a beautiful mansion, but not being able to climb the stairs because of heart trouble! How ironic to have everything you could want materially, but not have the ability to enjoy it. I read in the newspaper a couple of years ago about a woman who won the lottery, but who was dying of cancer. So many millions of pounds and yet it was of no value to her. All she wanted was her life.

God-centred, not wealth-centred

Jesus told a parable about being wealth-centred instead of God-centred:

> " 'I will do this: I will pull down my barns and build greater, and there I will store all my crops and my goods. And I will say to my soul, "Soul, you have many goods laid up for many years; take your ease; eat, drink, and be merry." ' But God said to him, 'Fool! This night your soul will be required of you; then whose will those things be which you have provided?' So is he who lays up treasure for himself, and is not rich toward God."
>
> (Luke 12:18–21)

Here is the key to wealth: to be God-focused, rich towards your heavenly Father. Here in Jesus' parable is a man who is self-centred and engrossed in doing things for his, and his family's, benefit. God does not come into the equation. God calls him a fool. Foolishness in biblical terms is nothing to do with immaturity or lack of education – a fool is someone who has no regard for God and who tries to take control of his own soul. God did not condemn this man because he had a ten-year plan. It's good to plan ahead. God didn't condemn him because he wanted to expand his business operations and increase his storage capacity. That's wise. God condemned the man because he believed that his money would provide him with spiritual security. God said to him, "You are a fool because you cannot buy salvation; you cannot buy a longer life. You don't realise that tonight you are going to die and all the things you have put your trust in will fall to someone else. Silly man!"

> **"We make excuses to God when things other than Him are our treasure, and we are too easily distracted by the stuff of life."**

A man's external prosperity is not evidence of his internal wealth. Jesus spoke of laying up treasure in heaven where no thief could conspire to take it away, where rust could not corrode it or moth consume it.

> *"For where your treasure is, there your heart will be also."*
>
> (Luke 12:34)

The question we must ask ourselves is: what are we planting in the seed beds of our hearts? Can anyone take away the treasure we have accumulated? Will life corrode it or consume it, or have we invested in the kind of treasure that will last forever?

Worldly treasure can come in many forms – for one person it may be money; another person will value their title and position more than money; another person again will invest everything they have in their relationship with another person. In fact, the three key reasons, in another parable of Jesus, that people gave for not being able to attend the Lord's great banquet were:

1. *Property*: "I've bought some land and I must go and view it..."
2. *Business interests*: "I have a new ox that I must try out..."
3. *People*: "I can't come, my wife doesn't want me to..."

We make excuses to God when things other than Him are our treasure, and we are too easily distracted by the stuff of life – things which should come *under God*, not before Him. Let us make a decision not to allow such things to control us and to be good stewards of all that God blesses us with.

We live in a world that is totally materialistic in its outlook, in which it is very easy to get sucked into the deceit of constantly being upwardly mobile. My advice to all Christian couples is this: never put one another under financial pressure you can't meet. The kind of thing I mean is: "Look, our friends have moved into a bigger house. Why can't we move to a bigger house?" or, "So and so has just had a conservatory ... when can we have one?" or, "Phil has just got himself a sports car. I'd really like to upgrade mine."

Of course, there is nothing intrinsically wrong in any of these things, unless, that is, it either pushes us beyond our means or stems from a wrong motivation.

If, in your daily living, you are always stretching beyond your reach, something in your attitude is wrong. As believers we need to learn to live within, or even below, our means.

Husbands: don't try to buy your wife's love. I meet too many men who mistakenly believe that if they don't give their wives everything they could ever want, they won't love them any more. What rubbish! Never buy what you cannot afford. Instead, wait until God prospers you.

Tithing and giving to God

Although many other books have been written on this subject, it would be remiss of me not to mention very briefly the subject of tithing and giving to God. I believe in tithing and giving. The main point I want to make about it is this: tithing and giving to God is primarily a Lordship issue, more than it is a money issue. We give to God out of our resources (which the Bible tells us actually belong to Him anyway) as an act of obedience because God wants to know He has captured our heart. He doesn't need our money!

Malachi 3:8-10 are key verses that show us God's economy for tithes and offerings:

> " 'Will a man rob God?
> Yet you have robbed Me!
> But you say,
> "In what way have we robbed You?"

In tithes and offerings.
You are cursed with a curse,
For you have robbed Me,
Even this whole nation.
Bring all the tithes into the storehouse,
That there may be food in My house,
And try Me now in this,'
Says the LORD of hosts,
'If I will not open for you the windows of heaven
And pour out for you such blessing
That there will not be room enough to receive it.' "

If you have not been giving to God out of your
resources – and I would include your time as well as
your money – then you have removed yourself from
under the canopy of God's blessing. You are actually
limiting what God is able to do for you in terms of
material blessing. God is so committed to His formula
of giving – give a small portion of what belongs to God
back to Him and you will receive multiplied blessings
in return – that it is one of the few places in Scripture
where God invites us to test Him out. If you are not
living in God's plan for your finances then you could
receive a £30,000 salary increase this year and still find
yourself poor and in debt! Why? Because you are trying
to operate outside of God's provision for you.

We all need to be faithful givers and to resource the
kingdom of God as God enables us. When we
understand that giving to God is a key that unlocks
immeasurable blessing and that God is just waiting to
prove that to us, then we may become more generous
with what is, after all, His money!

A revival church is a church of wealth – first spiritually, being relationally rich towards God and one another, and then financially, releasing wealth not simply to spend on itself, but to resource the work of God in its locality and to see the boundaries of the kingdom of God pushed forward. To be a revival church we need a wealth mentality born out of a right kingdom perspective. Let us be faithful in giving and see what God will do!

Wellbeing

A church that comes into revival will be made up of
people with a different mindset; people who think
differently about God, the Church, themselves, and
others. A revival person in a revival church is at peace
with God, themselves and those who they deal with in
life. They have a different mindset, different belief
patterns, because they have understood that they are
not just a member of a local church, but are part of a
living, active kingdom.

Shortly we will explore what it means to be at peace
with God, but before that, let me say that many more
believers need to see the bigger picture when it comes
to local church versus the kingdom of God. The first
thing we must all remember is that the Church belongs
to Jesus! He says, "I will build *My* Church." When
Jesus commissioned Peter He gave him the keys to the
kingdom, not the Church – a totally different concept –
and wherever the apostles travelled from then on, they
preached the message of the kingdom of God.
Wherever you and I travel on this earth we are
representatives of God's kingdom, demonstrating the
principles of His kingdom by the way we live and
conduct ourselves. We are ambassadors, messengers,
royal princes, warriors, whose job it is to proclaim the
advancement of God's kingdom on earth. It is out of

the kingdom and the people who are drawn into it through salvation that God then builds His Church.

After his commission, Peter was not planting a church, he was preaching the kingdom, and as he did so, thousands identified themselves with the call. "We want to be a part of that kingdom!" they cried. Out of that group of people Jesus founded His Church. Our job, therefore, as modern believers, is to preach Christ, crucified, resurrected and glorified. We are to establish God's kingdom on earth and to have kingdom priorities. Do you know it is possible to belong to a church and yet not be in the kingdom? You can be an Anglican and not be in the kingdom; a Baptist and not in the kingdom; a Methodist and not in the kingdom. We need to take our eyes off our inward looking concerns and grasp the big picture of what God wants to do in our nation. We need to be willing workers for the kingdom.

Wellbeing equals peace with God

When we become a Christian, the first phase of our changed nature takes place: we have peace with God. This is what I mean by "wellbeing". Suddenly, the world is a different place and we relate to it on an entirely different basis. As the hymn writer so aptly put it:

"Oh, the bliss of this glorious thought!
My sin, not in part but the whole,
Is nailed to the cross, and I bear it no more...
It is well, it is well, with my soul."

If you are in a revival church, then there must be a sense of peace with God. It distresses me that so many Christians I meet around the country do not have an abiding sense of God's peace in their lives, because the peace of God is freely offered and given to all who have put their trust in Jesus.

> **"There are two things that God is very keen to deal with: trouble and fear. He does not want His people to be afraid."**

Jesus came to release to us the peace of God that surpasses all human understanding (Philippians 4:7). That does not mean that we are given some "magical" protection from the trials of life, which all of us have to endure, but God's peace enables us to "live above" the trials and to navigate them successfully.

When Jesus ascended into heaven He left us one of the greatest gifts we could ever receive, apart from the Holy Spirit. He said,

> *"Peace I leave with you, My peace I give to you; not as the world gives do I give to you. Let not your heart be troubled, neither let it be afraid."*
>
> (John 14:27)

This tells us that our spiritual wellbeing features very high on Jesus' list of concerns for us. This verse also tells us that there are two things that God is very keen to deal with: trouble and fear. He does not want His people to be afraid. His peace is designed to dispel fear. People in revival are not dogged by fears and troubles all the time, they are blessed and free. Jesus never commands us to do something we are not capable of, and so when He says, "Let not your heart be troubled and do not be afraid" we can safely assume we are capable of doing that. What we need, is to focus our attention on Jesus and look to Him as the source of all we need.

The Greek word for "peace" in this verse also means "quietness, rest and prosperity". To have a *quietness* about our Spirit means we have grasped the imperative, *"Be still, and know that I am God"* (Psalm 46:10).

Wellbeing also equals *rest*. We go about our work for the Lord starting from a place of rest in Him. Busyness is more to do with who you are than what you actually do. Some people can be doing five things at once and yet be at peace. Others can be doing just one thing and it stresses them out. Why? Because God's peace and rest is an internal quality. Personally, I would much rather be busy and active for God. We all have different metabolisms and some people are naturally more energetic than others, but I feel for people who have to be in bed before 10.00pm each night and don't get up until 8.00am the next morning. It strikes me that when they die they'll have been asleep for almost half their life! Frank Houston used to say that research had shown that the majority of people die in bed, so he intended to keep out of bed as much as possible!

Jesus tells us not to be troubled or agitated about anything because the third thing that the peace of God does for us is give us *prosperity*. He assures us that He will take care of all our needs, so we no longer need to be anxious about our future, as most people are.

When the peace of God is at work inside you it is literally transforming. It is like switching on a light where previously there was darkness. It begins to grow inside you and the sense of wellbeing washes over your soul. It is produced by knowing for certain that you are reconciled to God and have eternal hope in Christ.

Some people come to me and tell me that they don't feel at peace. The first thing I tell them is this: you must be living in peace with God before you can live in *the* peace of God. In other words, we must repent of any sin that is causing a blockage and preventing God's peace from flowing freely in us, and also we must avoid continually striving – striving for acceptance, for God's favour, to justify ourselves – all things which Christ has already accomplished for us through the cross!

God's peace releases us from the bondage of continual striving to attain perfection. Of course we can have godly goals and values that we aim for in life – that's vital. But we need not have the kind of driven spirit that leaves us wide open and vulnerable as soon as we let down our defences.

Wellbeing equals unity

When you are in a revival church and know the sense of wellbeing that God's peace brings, nothing is too much trouble. The active work of the Holy Spirit brings people of faith into a quality of relationship that far surpasses anything that human ingenuity could engineer. When the peace of God is absent, the church is wide open to attack and trouble. Church splits occur, people get offended over issues that should be easily resolvable, and there are continual rumours about "murmuring" among the people. The peace of God does away with all of this and brings unity.

In Acts 2:1 we read of Jesus' disciples that,

> "When the Day of Pentecost had fully come, they were all with one accord in one place."

The phrase "with one accord" means they were unanimous in their intent and had a unity of purpose. A phrase that crops up several times as the story of the early Church unfolds after Pentecost underlines this fact:

> "It seemed good to us, being assembled with one accord, to send chosen men to you with our beloved Barnabas and Paul..."
>
> (Acts 15:25)

> "It seemed good to the Holy Spirit, and to us, to lay upon you no greater burden than these necessary things..."
>
> (Acts 15:28)

A revival church can make decisions that are good and correct as the leadership is "tuned in" to the Holy

Spirit. When each person in a leadership team is listening carefully to God's voice, they can quickly come to a place of agreement on issues and will have one mind and purpose. The peace of God leads to a harmony of purpose that leads to action. Some churches, like some local government agencies, never seem to make the critical decisions that need making for two reasons: first, they fail to reach a place of unity and peace among themselves, and second, they are too busy trying to please all of the people all of the time, instead of listening to and carrying out God's mandate.

A friend of mine who pastored a church in Scotland reported to a church board who had the final say on all major decisions in church life. They once took six months to decide whether they should increase the capacity of their toilets from one cubicle to two! We can laugh about things like this, but actually, it's disgraceful! Do you think there is going to be a revival in that church? I seriously doubt it. No wonder my friend eventually left, very frustrated and became the pastor of another church.

A group of people who are overcome with wellbeing know where they are going and get things done. The Bible says of the early believers that,

> *"All who believed were together, and had all things in common."*
>
> (Acts 2:44)

There was a consistency about these people that is often lacking in churches today. Unless we are truly living in peace with God, we will never connect properly with other people. These believers were of one accord. Any church that can reach this place is unstoppable. Notice there was no individualism here – the people were together with all things in common. This was not British isolationism! The Christian life is intended to be one of relationship with Jesus first and foremost, a relationship with other believers next, and then a relationship with a disenfranchised world. Your Christianity is flawed if you have no desire to be a friend to other people or to be accountable for your actions.

Wellbeing equals a passion for the cause

When Liverpool won the European Cup in 2005 there was an outpouring of emotion and elation from their fans that was breathtaking in its intensity and fervour. Thousands of fans made the trip to Istanbul to see the match. People ducked out of work to go, some were even reported to have lied to their wives, so fanatical were they about supporting their team. Following the victory it was reported that 750,000 people took a day off work to throng in the streets of the city and welcome the players home. It shows us what an incredible epidemic football has become in our nation.

When was last time the church brought a city centre to a standstill and needed the police to intervene to direct the traffic? Why don't we march through the streets of our towns waving banners and letting everyone know about the great victory that Jesus has won? These things tell me that we are not really in revival. If we are in revival, then heaven help us! The world is in revival to football, but it's not happening in the Church yet. Liverpool's previous manager said, "Football isn't life and death ... it's more important than that!" And a couple of years ago Sky TV advertised football with the slogan, "It's our religion and we're proud of it." What is our problem in the Church then? I believe it is that we have not truly committed ourselves to relationship with one another in pursuit of the common goals of the kingdom.

Acts 4:32 says,

> *"Now the multitude of those who believed were of one heart and one soul; neither did anyone say that any of the things he possessed was his own, but they had all things in common."*

(Acts 4:32)

"The apostles were able to move in such power because they were supported by the unity of the people."

The early believers had all things in common and pooled their assets to achieve their goals. Some people get uncomfortable when I am preaching this message because they don't really want to be in covenant with other believers. They prefer to keep a bit of distance and preserve their individualism. But we will never see revival without forging an unbreakable unity and commonality of purpose among us! The following verse says that,

> "With great power the apostles gave witness to the resurrection of the Lord Jesus. And great grace was upon them all."
>
> (Acts 4:33)

I believe that the apostles were able to move in such power because they were supported by the unity of the people. They were liberated because the people were of one accord. As we see our churches deepen in unity and the peace of God I believe we will see more power from the platform! Often the power from the pulpit is restricted to the extent that the pews will tolerate! If we want to see more miracles in our churches then we need churches populated with people of faith who will believe God for the miraculous.

Along with a release of power, the wellbeing that results from the peace of God will also bring *provision.* In Acts we read,

> "Nor was there anyone among them who lacked; for all who were possessors of lands or houses sold them, and brought the proceeds of the things that were sold, and laid them at the apostles' feet; and they were distributed to each as anyone had need."
>
> (Acts 4:34–35)

What an amazing picture of unity! In our own church we have a programme called Helping Hands that provides food for the poor. We do this because we believe that caring for others should be a routine part of church life. Any church in revival will have as a core value a ministry to the poor. We have to care for people and love them with God's love. As the family of God we must also care for one another. This is a church in revival: where the family of God share their resources, meet one another's needs and reach out to others.

Wellbeing equals boldness!

As the power of the Holy Spirit swept through the early Church incredible things happened: healings occurred; the gospel was preached with authority and power; thousands were saved and added to the church daily – not weekly – daily!

> *"And when they had prayed, the place where they were assembled together was shaken; and they were all filled with the Holy Spirit, and they spoke the word of God with boldness."*
>
> (Acts 4:31)

Not only did this wellbeing bring peace, unity and a passion for the cause of the kingdom, but it also brought a boldness to the believers. The Christians were no longer a band of scared misfits, hiding out and trying to dodge the authorities; they were fearless and they moved in the power of the Spirit doing all the things Jesus previously did.

Often when I travel around the country I see in the Church a timidity that is frightening. Sometimes people have commented to me, "I bet you don't preach like that in your own church!" but the fact is, I do! I like to tell people the truth, straight and unembellished, because people respond to bold, truthful people. Recently a businessman who had joined our church told me, "I come here because you preach straight down the line. You preach with love, but you never pull any punches. As a successful businessman, I need that protection!"

The wellbeing of God results in boldness. The Holy Spirit is capable of transforming us from timid, feeble believers into God-fearing, power-filled Christians who know their kingdom mandate from God and carry it out uncompromisingly. The early Church's believers were full of peace, truth, wonders, unity, and they received this boldness. The Greek word for it is *parresia* and also means outspokenness, to have a freedom of speech, a cheerful courage.

It grieves me how many Christians have a lack of moral courage. They avoid telling the truth; they talk behind other people's backs; they very rarely deal with issues with true integrity; and they tend to blame other people for their problems! This is not the way that members of the Christian community should behave. We need to be bold and face up to our problems. The believers in Acts lived in relationship with one another in a context of truth. The Holy Spirit had changed their hearts and minds. Such behaviour was anathema to them.

I wonder how many churches experience this kind of

situation on a weekly basis, but are afraid to deal with
it properly? A lady comes up to one of the leaders and
says, "God has told me that I should be leading the
worship." Now, the leader knows full well that this
lady is tone deaf and couldn't keep a tambourine in
tune, never mind anything else, but apparently God
has told her she is gifted to lead! What does he do?
What happens in the average church? "Hmm, well let's
pray about that and see what God says." No! This is the
wrong thing to do and it's cowardly. If you pussyfoot
around with people like that and then let them down
they will not thank you in the long run. We need to
have the courage to tell people the truth: "Sorry love,
but you can't sing! However, you're great at cooking,
why don't you help with the catering at the next
event?"

Without meaning to be offensive I don't want to
go to any more churches where there is an old biddy
playing the piano who has been there for the last forty
years and the leaders won't replace her in case she
leaves the church! Everyone knows she can't play well,
but nobody will admit it. Could these be the same
churches that are populated by the people who always
say, "Lovely message, Pastor" at the end of every
service, even if they hated it? We don't have to be rude
to one another, but we should at least tell the truth
to one another! Christians should be the most upfront
people in the world. Bosses should be able to come to
Christians on their workforce and say to them, "I'm
asking you this because I know you will tell me the
truth . . . " Sadly, Christians often don't have this
reputation.

The first believers in the Church looked very different from this. They told one another the truth. They met together and broke bread, lived with an attitude of forgiveness, and dealt with problems before they became issues. They met with one another from house to house and placed a high value on relationships. Probably not many of them could cook exotic meals, but they had simple food based around fellowship. Houses were not full of loose, idle talk, but were self-controlled and prayerful. They continued in the apostles' doctrine and there was structure without suffocation. This is how the Church should look today.

Wellbeing equals an end to blame shifting

The final result of seeing the wellbeing of God among us in a revival church is an end to blame shifting, where every believer takes responsibility for their own spirituality and is accountable for the way they live. This is a godly, biblical community functioning at its best.

> **"A revival church is only as good as the righteousness of its people!"**

A revival church is only as good as the righteousness of its people! Too many Christians are quick to blame others for the state of their walk with God instead of taking responsibility for it themselves. Our spirituality is not the responsibility of our cell group leader or our pastor – we are personally accountable to God. I know people who have backslidden because they felt depressed and then blamed their fellow cell group members for not phoning them. Maybe those people should have phoned that person to see where they were and how they were doing – but that does not excuse the bad attitude of the person themselves. Their walk with God is their responsibility. It's time we stopped making petty excuses and asked God to adjust our heart attitudes.

Again, if our children are going off the rails spiritually, whose responsibility is it? It's ours! It's not the pastor's fault, the cell group leader's fault, or the youth worker's fault. All these people are there to assist us, but unless we take responsibility ourselves their input will have limited value.

Examining the state of our hearts

I believe that a key factor in helping us to examine our hearts and to get rid of a blame shifting culture is to elevate the importance of communion. Most of us will take communion on a weekly basis, but I suspect that often we don't give it the time it deserves. Whilst communion must never become a legalistic ritual, neither must it be marginalised. It is the only corporate function of the Church that has direct commands and consequences attached to it.

What other activity in church life brings us into such close contact with the sacrifice of the Lord Jesus for the salvation of our souls? It is a call to remember Him and to affirm the new covenant in His blood. The Bible issues a warning to us that all those who partake of this sacrament in an unworthy manner bring judgement on themselves. If you do that, it's self-harm, there is nobody to blame but yourself. The apostle Paul put it very bluntly:

"He who eats and drinks in an unworthy manner eats and drinks judgement to himself."

(1 Corinthians 11:29)

The consequences of this "judgement" are plain to see, Paul says:

"For this reason many are weak and sick among you, and many sleep..."

(1 Corinthians 11:30)

If any of us are feeling weak and sick, a good place to begin to counteract that is by examining our attitude towards communion. Some believers are sick because of their attitude towards fellowship with other believers. They have unresolved issues, grudges and grievances towards brother and sisters, refuse to deal with them before God, and yet still go ahead and share communion. This is not right! Christians who do this are eating and drinking judgement upon themselves. Paul calls it "failing to discern the Lord's body" (see verse 29). He means we show no respect for the Body of Christ, the fellowship of believers. The resulting disunity can actually cause us to become sick, or worse, according to Paul, to die prematurely!

It is a harsh word, but nevertheless the Bible puts it before us: some believers will "fall asleep", which is a euphemism for "die", before their time if they abuse communion and so disrespect the Body of Christ. It is strong language and shows how seriously God takes this act of remembrance regarding His Son's sacrifice.

How do we avoid such judgement? Self-inspection in cooperation with the Holy Spirit is the prime action. How much better it is to allow the Holy Spirit to chasten and correct us than to act in a rebellious manner. The Bible teaches that judgement begins with the house of God – you and me – we are convicted and corrected, so that we do not receive judgement as the world does.

If our lifestyle is wrong, then we need to take steps to correct it. We can only blame ourselves, so we must take responsibility, repent and change. Sin always tries to mitigate our responsibility, but the buck stops with us. King David modelled for us the correct attitude and found release in telling the truth:

> *"Against You, You only, have I sinned . . .*
> *Create in me a clean heart, O God,*
> *And renew a steadfast spirit within me."*
>
> (Psalm 51:4, 10)

If we are going to build revival churches in our nation we have to be a church that thrives on wellbeing, stops blaming others for our level of spirituality, stops moaning about what the church is like, and makes it into what it can be! We have got to develop men and women of integrity. Integrity does not start with others – it starts with us!

If we would enact this then there would be no offended people in our churches, there would be no spirit of criticism. We must put these things to death. We can choose life or death; we can choose what our heart attitudes will be. Only God has the power to start a revival, but you and I are capable of stifling it. We must put away our childish attitudes, as the apostle Paul said, and cooperate with God's purposes for our generation. Then we may be blessed enough to see a great revival bringing glory to Christ's name.

Note _____

1. Words by Horatio G. Spafford, 1873. Music by Philip P. Bliss, 1876.

Conclusion

Some readers will ask, "Why was prayer not one of the five attributes?" Well, in my innocence I have assumed that any Christian or church worthy of the name of Jesus is committed to prayer.

Prayer is the lubricant on which Worship, Word, Wonders, Wealth and Wellbeing function. Prayer should be as normal as a young child beginning to mimic his/her parents and then developing a vocabulary, thus enabling a conversation of relationship and love. With over 232 scriptures on prayer alone the Bible is full of the need of a two-way conversation with the Almighty. We are to *"pray without ceasing"* (1 Thessalonians 5:17).

James 5:16 is a powerful verse:

1. Confess your faults one to another
2. Pray one for another
3. That we may be healed
4. Effectual, fervent prayer from a righteous man avails much.

Prayer may play an integral part in revival. Wesley believed implicitly in prayer and fasting. Yet, where there is no worship, prayer will be scarce and where no desire for the Word is found, prayer is based on emotion. When signs and wonders abound it is mainly indicative of the underpinning of prayer. Few live in true abundance without personal relationship with the Provider. Without the daily conversation with the Lord in the cool of the day there can be little contentment.

Another question: "Why is intercession not one of the five as many are engaged in this ministry are seeking revival?" Well, hold on to your hats!

The New Testament gives no indication of such a ministry or gift! Christ Himself has become our Intercessor. Hebrews 7 speaks of Jesus being our intercessor and High Priest – neither office is now held by man. God manifested in the Son and Holy Spirit (Romans 8:26–27) now stands in the gap for us, the cross completing not only our salvation, but placing on His shoulders the government of His eternal kingdom.

So many faltering with the pressure of "standing in the gap" will be encouraged that God the Father found One who could and who did!

1 Timothy 2:1 may on the face of it endorse the act of human intercession. It is, however, a challenge to fervency of prayer, not *on behalf* of others, but *for* others.

I trust that your quest for the kingdom of God to come in full power and glory to your town or city has been challenged by the thoughts in this book. Until revival, be renewed and don't let anybody persuade you to reject your destiny. John the Baptist wanted to deter Jesus from being baptised on the basis that he felt unworthy to be used. How often have we tried to thwart the will of God by false modesty? Jesus, however, would not allow anything, or anybody, to restrict His future.

"I must fulfil all righteousness."

(Matthew 3:15)

For a true revival the following, reflected in Jesus' act of baptism, needs to transpire:

1. **Obedience.** Jesus stood in the waters of death – death to self-will. The cup of suffering could not pass by. He had to drink of it for our redemption, for us to see the glory of God. The obedience of self-denial: *"not my will but yours be done"*, must be faced.
2. **The heavens opened.** Good preaching, great worship and family activities can draw crowds, but only an open heaven will connect to the throne room of our Lord. It becomes easy when the clouds of doubt have been dismissed.
3. **The voice of the Father gave endorsement to the Son.** When the Lord is "well pleased" with us and He commands that the people *"hear us"*, we see miracles in the name of Jesus.
4. **The Holy Spirit descended as a dove.** The fire is great, it purges, purifies and perfects, yet the dove brings peace.

It is well with my soul...

It seems good to us and the Holy Spirit...

*"Peace I leave with you, My peace I give to you;
not as the world gives do I give to you. Let not your
heart be troubled, neither let it be afraid."*

(John 14:27)

See you in the blessing!

About the Author

David Carr has been involved in the ministry of the Gospel for over thirty years, travelling extensively throughout the world. David is the Senior Minister of Renewal Christian Centre, Solihull, UK, which he pioneered in 1972 and which is now one of the largest Spirit-filled churches in the UK.

Renewal is affiliated to the Free Methodist Church of the UK and North America. Prior to this David was an Executive Member of the Elim Pentecostal Church.

As well as being a local pastor for many years, his experience within the world of professional football, where he managed 700 of the country's leading players, has enabled David to relate to people from all walks of life. He is in great demand as a conference speaker both in the UK and abroad and regularly conducts leadership conferences.

David has a strong prophetic ministry and moves in the gifts of the Holy Spirit. Over recent years many signs, wonders and miracles have been apparent during and after the preaching of the Word. Recently there has been an incredible move of the Holy Spirit within the church which has resulted in many healings and an awesome presence of God.

David is married to Molly and they have three children, Ashley, Melanie and Lucy.

We hope you enjoyed reading this New Wine book.
For details of other New Wine books
and a range of 2,000 titles from other
Word and Spirit publishers visit our website:
www.newwineministries.co.uk